# Linguistics for Teaching English in Multilingual Classrooms

Sarina Chugani Molina

# DEDICATION

This book is dedicated to my parents, Mr. Gobind Chugani and the late, Mrs. Sunita Chugani. Your life experiences have nurtured in me the curiosity to learn about the various cultures and languages of the world. My husband, Larry Molina and children, Mina and Sai Molina– thank you for your kindness, patience and understanding.

To all of my students past, present, and future - your dedication and passion for Teachers of English to Speakers of Other Languages serves as the inspiration behind this book.

# CONTENTS

# ACKNOWLEDGMENTS

This book would not have been possible without the years of teaching and learning interactions I have had with English learners in schools, community colleges, language academies and community programs within the U.S. and abroad. I have learned much from my students, both graduate students who spent countless hours working with English learners in the field and from my own English learners, who I have had the opportunity to teach over the last 20 years. A special thank you goes to Paulina Saravia Castillón and Miriam Voth for spending countless hours reviewing and providing editorial comments on this book.

# 1 INTRODUCTION

In my experiences teaching linguistics, teacher candidates have been most apprehensive about this particular course. One reason for the apprehension may be a flashback experience they encounter when they hear the word "linguistics" and are transported back to their grammar classroom, where memories of their sense of inadequacy about their grammar knowledge prevail. Another reason is often the assumption they sense about the disconnect between the concepts of linguistics and teaching their particular content area courses. They may wonder, "How is this relevant to teaching math?" or "How is this relevant to teaching academic reading or writing?" However, after understanding the context of their increasingly diverse classrooms and the role of language in making content comprehensible, teacher candidates begin to unravel the important role that language plays in communicating and negotiating meaning with their students in every subject area.

In presenting the field of linguistics in pieces that teacher candidates can relate to and apply in their daily work with their students, they often report feeling more comfortable with the content and appreciate the ways in which this knowledge will enhance their work in meeting the needs of their linguistically diverse students.

The statistic for teachers leaving the teaching profession in their first few years of teaching is quite striking. Some attribute this to the lack of preparation they have in order to better support the needs of their multilingual and multi-cultural students. As a teacher educator today working to prepare future teachers who work in the K-12 sector as well as in the field of TESOL, I find that it is important for teachers to be equipped with the necessary skills to appreciate linguistic and cultural diversity in this global and interconnected world.

Linda Darling-Hammond (1997) captures this sentiment in the following passage.

> Meeting the challenge of cultural diversity is an agenda that is central to today's quest to develop schools that can educate all students for the challenging world they face – a world that is both more technologically and more multiculturally rich and more complex than ever before in our history. The work of educating educators is, at root, the work that will enable us to sustain a productive and pluralistic democracy, for it is the capacities of teachers that make democratic education possible – that is, an education that enables all people to find and act on who they are; what their passions, gifts, and talents may be; and how they want to make a contribution to each other and the world (Darling-Hammond, 1997, p. viii).

There are many books on the topic of understanding and approaching cultural differences in the classroom, but very little on understanding the needs of students from multilingual backgrounds. The purpose of this book is to help teacher candidates understand the nature of language and linguistic differences and how to approach the linguistic needs of their students from a socio-culturally sensitive space.

This book integrates the essential theoretical background in the field of linguistics with practical exercises and tried and tested activities for classroom application. Each chapter begins with an introduction to the fundamental concepts within each area of linguistics, namely phonetics, phonology, morphology, syntax, semantics and pragmatics. Each chapter concludes with exercises and activities for classroom application to support student learning in each of these areas of linguistics. A glossary is provided at the end of the book, where you are encouraged to define linguistic terminology and concepts in your own words with personal and relevant examples to help solidify your understanding of these terms.

# 2 THE STUDY OF LANGUAGE

To date, there are between 6800-7000 identified languages spoken in the world today. There are many more that have yet to be discovered. Language is one of the most magnificent capacities that human beings possess. It is a means through which we communicate shared understanding, new knowledge and hand this knowledge down to successive generations. In other words, language helps us to leave a mark. *Language* supports the human desire to communicate and negotiate meaning. It is innate, complex, dynamic and in many ways, quite arbitrary. *Linguistics* is a field that looks at the complex nature of language through systematic investigation. Through empirical research, linguists shed light on the structure and use of language. In this chapter, we will review the various attributes of language, followed by a brief introduction to first and second language acquisition theories in order to shed light on the complexity of the language learning process, particularly in acquiring a second or additional language.

## Language as Innate

The desire to communicate is innate in most, if not all, human beings. As soon as children are born, they begin to communicate (e.g. cry) with their caretakers to meet their immediate needs of hunger or discomfort. As they grow, they begin to smile, laugh, and coo to interact with their caretakers. The caretakers in turn encourage this interaction through nonverbal and verbal responses. As the child begins to speak, the caretakers, older siblings and community members support the child's language development by providing feedback through their interactions. Through this process, the child matures into a fully proficient participant in that particular linguistic community. As such, the language learning process for children is subconscious, innate and natural.

## Language as Complex

Children begin speaking one to two word sentences early on and multi-word sentences by the age of 2 or 3. As they grow, they begin to move from the more concrete, "here and now" language, to more abstract concepts. What makes language complex is that from the linguistic toolbox that children have acquired over time, they continuously create novel sentences, ones they may have not heard spoken before. Let's take the following words: "I" "mama" "want" "milk" "juice" "apple." Initially, a child may use one word to express his need. He may just say, "milk" to express his desire for milk. Then, he may include two words as he gains more command of the language structure and say, "Mama, milk." As he moves into multi-word sentences, he may begin to say, "I want milk." As he learns new words, he may be able to switch out the nouns and say, "I want juice." or "Mama, I want apple." Gradually, he will begin to create novel sentences to express his thoughts, opinions and needs.

## Language as Dynamic

Language continues to change to meet the needs for communication. With progress in technology and global communication, language had to keep up with the shifting needs of the times. Facebook invented the term "poke" when one wants to engage in conversation with another user, or simply let them know that they are thinking of them. Google has created a variety of modalities to meet the communication and collaborative needs of the changing world, such as "Google drive" and "Google docs." This evolutionary trajectory of language is what makes it dynamic. Likewise, pockets of linguistic communities have evolved within larger linguistic communities. For example, it may be difficult to understand the language used by adolescents. Although this may be different today, at one point the words "bad" and "sick" bore a positive connotation amongst adolescents in the United States, rather than negative as in their original, intended semantic composition. People within particular careers or jobs have language that is shared and understood within these micro-linguistic communities. Such micro-communities can also be found amongst people who share similar interests such as in the surfing or gaming communities.

## Language as Arbitrary

When we hear the word "dog," we all may have different images that come to mind, which are often based on our previous experiences with dogs. What we share in common in response to hearing the word "dog," is the *conceptual* or mental *image*, which includes an animal with four legs, fur, and perhaps pointy ears, similar to a fox or wolf. Our *referent* or real world *image* would be images that come to mind based on our previous experiences or a current dog we may know. The form or symbol has various representations. In Japanese, the word for dog is "inu," with various character representations as in 犬 (Chinese character) and いぬ (Japanese hiragana alphabet). In Hindi, the term is "kutta" represented as कुत्ता in Devanagiri script. Dog itself is a very abstract term with no connection to the animal itself. The same can be said for the words "table," "book," "dance" and so on. However, there are some words often associated with sounds that resemble their referent or real world concepts such as "pitter-patter" to describe the sound of rain or "ring" to describe the sound of an incoming call or a verb to mean to call, used more often in British English than American English. These are called *onomatopoetic words*. Animal sounds are also considered onomatopoetic sounds though some seem more arbitrary than others. In Japanese, a rooster cries, "ko ke kokkou," in English, "cock-a-doodle-doo," and "kikirikí" in Spanish none of which resemble the sound of an actual rooster. Some languages are laden with these words particularly within literary pieces of work. Some symbolic representations of words could also be more closely related to their corresponding real world objects than how they are actually pronounced. For example, in Chinese, the character for tree is 木, which can be argued to resemble a tree. Adding an additional tree 林 represents the woods, where a few more trees can be found, and adding yet another tree 森 represents the forest, where many more trees can be found.

## First Language Acquisition

Children are often said to learn their mother tongue naturally or through a subconscious process. Initially, in order to understand the process of language acquisition, researchers thought that children learned through repetition and imitation. B. F. Skinner, a theorist in the field of behavioral psychology, described learning as a process of *operant conditioning*, where through repetitive signals in the environment and positive reinforcement learning can occur. Through rigorous research, Noam Chomsky, world-renowned linguist, found patterns in the ways in which children develop and acquire particular units of language. Through his analysis and research of these patterns, he postulated that children do not learn merely through repetition or conditioning because they had consistent errors that were common across all children learning their first language. For example, children would say "goed*" or "eated*" before they learned their irregular forms "went" and "ate." If it is the case and they do not hear these forms occurring naturally in their environment, Chomsky believed that there must be some other mechanism involved in language acquisition. He called this the *Language Acquisition Device* (LAD). This conceptual black box, he believed, was responsible for registering and formulating rules based on the input received from the environment. When children say, "goed*," they are overgeneralizing the past tense ending for verbs to all verbs before formulating exception rules for irregular verbs.

Children are said to be able to differentiate between their mother tongue and another language before they are even born. Around six to about eight months of age, they begin repetitive consonant-vowel sound patterns to communicate their needs. For example, they may learn to say "mama" for mother or "baba" for bottle. Then, between the ages of nine months to about a year and a half, they can begin to produce single word utterances. Between this time and about two years of age, children are able to create two word sentences around what is called a pivot word. They can learn and use for example, "all gone," but are not able to differentiate between these two words and recognize it as one unit. You may hear them say, "Juice allgone" or "Cheerio allgone." Usually between two to about two and a half years of age, they may still use two word sentences, but have a better vocabulary in terms of nouns, adjectives, and verbs. For example, they may say "sister hungry" or "flower pretty." After this time period, children's language blossoms into multiword sentences that continue to increase in complexity as the child grows up.

## Second or Additional Language Acquisition

Second language acquisition (or any additional language after the acquisition of the first language) has been a fascinating topic for many researchers and language learners alike. This is because there is a definite recognition that there are some differences between how one learns a first and second or additional language. Stephen Krashen, in his eclectic model of second language acquisition, identifies five broad areas that describe the process of acquiring a second or additional language, and serves as a good introduction to understanding theories in second language acquisition.

### Acquisition-Learning Hypothesis

Krashen first differentiates between first and second language acquisition, where he postulates that first language acquisition is a subconscious process where children acquire the language through a natural desire to communicate and express themselves. The child usually is immersed in an environment where the language is heard and has caretakers (i.e. mothers, fathers, siblings, babysitters, teachers) who serve as models of the language and provide supports to help the child become a member of the linguistic community. In learning a second or additional language, theorists recognize that it appears to be a more conscious process, where understanding grammar rules and knowledge of the structure of the language is often useful, whereas to a young child, such knowledge is often not meaningful in their language learning process.

## Monitor Hypothesis

Just like the verb "to monitor," the monitor hypothesis is a theory that describes the process by which a person self-corrects their utterances based on the feedback they receive from their environment. When language learners overuse their monitor or self-editing system, they often produce sporadic, choppy sentences because they are so concerned about the "correctness" of their utterances. On the other end of the spectrum, we have language learners who do not self-correct at all and produce utterances with errors throughout. Over time, however, these utterances become quite difficult to correct and can become what linguists call "fossilized." As with dinosaur bones, which become fossils after centuries and are difficult to excavate, the same they believe applies to language that has been used incorrectly and left unaddressed for many years. Now, it is important that during the initial stages of language learning that the focus is on fluency because too much focus on accuracy during these initial periods can lead to halting speech and fear of speaking. However, as the language learners move from initial stages of proficiency to advanced levels, then focus on accuracy becomes important.

Here, it is important to note that there is a difference between a *mistake* or slip and an *error*. A mistake or slip can be self-corrected, where the language learner knows the rule, but due to some type of stress such as time constraints imposed on their responses, they may produce incorrect utterances. An error on the other hand is one that the language learner is not able to self-correct because the rule has not been acquired as yet. These errors are ones that teachers should focus on and address through mini-grammar lessons by bringing these rules to their language learners' consciousness. Integrating grammar instruction through meaningful themes rather than in isolation can make grammar learning a more meaningful and relevant learning experience for the students. Ideally, we would want our language learners to be optimal monitor users, where they neither under use nor over use their monitors.

## Natural Order Hypothesis

In looking at how children acquire first language segments, theorists such as Noam Chomsky found that they follow a particular order of acquisition, which often holds true in second or additional language acquisition. For example, children would often over-apply or generalize the [-ed] past tense ending rule to all past tense verbs before they acquire their irregular forms. For example, we would hear children say, "goed*" or "eated*" before they learn their irregular forms, "went" and "ate." Similar patterns of acquisition are also reported in the acquisition of second or additional languages.

## Input Hypothesis

Just like we will not be able to understand complex engineering concepts without having foundational knowledge in mathematical concepts, it is believed that language can be learned when the knowledge presented is within the vicinity of the language learner's current level of understanding. The language learner's current level is represented as "i" and the level they can grasp next is represented as "i+1." In order for language to be comprehensible, it cannot be at levels far beyond their current level ( i ) such as i+20 or 30. It should be closer to the learner's current level of understanding. Lev Vygotsky, a Russian psychologist, described this similar phenomenon as Zone of Proximal Development (ZPD). Mothers and caretakers provide this type of scaffolded support to their children as they are picking up the language and help to make meaning comprehensible. For example, when the child says, "I goed to the park today," the mother might say, "Oh, you went to the park today" with an emphasis on went. When the child actually registers this new knowledge and it is within their ZPD, they will slowly, but surely self-correct and acquire this irregular form. In the classroom in terms of language learning, teachers and even fellow classmates can often serve as models of the language and scaffold the language learning process for their students and peers.

It is important to note that in addition to the input hypothesis and working on the receptive skills, theorist, Merrill Swain, postulates the importance of productive skills, which she termed the "output hypothesis." She believed that it was important for language learners to produce language and ascertain its correctness based on feedback from the hearers of the language. She theorizes that producing language has three important functions for language learning. One function includes the possibility of noticing errors in their utterance. If, for example, the person with whom you are speaking raises their eyebrow or is puzzled by your utterance, you may do a quick cross-check of your utterance and find or not find the root of the issue that has contributed to the failure in communicating your intended meaning. Second, in addition to the important opportunity for noticing one's errors, producing language or output can allow the speaker to test their knowledge of the language, what Swain refers to as "hypothesis testing." According to Richard Schmidt, when and only when one recognizes or notices one's errors, will there be potential for learning and acquiring some aspect of the language that has not been acquired thus. Lastly, output also serves a third purpose, a metalinguistic function, in terms of helping learners think about their language skills and internalize rules they gauge from the input they receive.

## Affective Filter Hypothesis

The belief behind this hypothesis is that low anxiety, high self-confidence and high-motivation, facilitates the process of language learning. Though research has shown that some anxiety can be facilitative in learning, too much anxiety may be debilitative. For example, if you were called on in class to answer a question, did not know the answer at that time and experienced some sense of embarrassment, then it is possible that you will never forget that question or answer for a long time to come. Likewise, if your losing word in a spelling bee competition is "broccoli," you may never forget the spelling henceforth due to the extreme pressure and anxiety caused by misspelling the word in a public forum. There are however, many more affective variables that may play a key role in the language learning process such as a learner's aptitude, metacognitive skills, ambiguity tolerance, willingness to communicate amongst other such internal and external factors.

Understanding the complexity of language and the language learning process is an important foundation for recognizing and approaching the linguistic needs of your English learners.

**EXERCISES**

Answer the following questions:

1) Describe the process of first language acquisition. How is it similar to or different from how adults learn a second or additional language?

2) Describe Krashen's theory of second language acquisition. Then, think about ways of applying 2-3 of these theories in the language learning classroom or your subject area. For example, in terms of the monitor hypothesis, you may want to consider how you would approach error correction as a teacher.

3) How could you approach grammar instruction in a meaningful way?

4) How would you approach error correction with the knowledge of the theoretical foundations of language learning and acquisition?

## CLASSROOM APPLICATION

Meaningful grammar instruction can happen in many ways in the classroom. One of the best ways to select the grammar points you would like to teach in a mini-lesson would be to first differentiate your student's mistakes from their errors. According to Corder's (1967) study on language errors, *errors* are defined as those that interfere with meaning or can lead to communication breakdown. Learners have not acquired the forms as yet. On the other hand, he defines *mistakes*, as slips of forms that the learner is able to self-correct. Mistakes often occur when the learner has cognitive overload or is nervous. Then using your student's written work or speech segments, create a mini-grammar lesson addressing their needs using authentic examples from their work. This is a more powerful way to address their needs in this area and support them in noticing their own errors. Chances are that if they see it, hear it, and apply it in their own work, they will acquire this language feature over time through practice and monitoring these areas in their own work.

For example, if a significant number of students in your class are having issues with subject-verb agreement, it would be important to share the rule with them and then have them self-correct their own written pieces. Instead of having students conjugate a list of pre-selected verbs in the following way, "I play, You play, He/She/It plays, We play, You (plural) play and They play," you can share one slide with the rule on verb conjugation and select subjects and verbs from your students' work to demonstrate the conjugation rules. Lastly, you can indicate in one or two instances, ways in which to make the subject and verb agree in their written pieces, but then have them correct the rest on their own.

7

# 3 PHONETICS

*Phonetics* is the study of sounds. In the English language, we have 26 letters in the alphabet, but 44 or more sounds depending on different dialectical variations. For example, there are different ways in which to pronounce the letter [a]. When teaching English learners and also young children the alphabet, teachers may initially differentiate the letter [a] as long [a] (eɪ) and short [a] (æ) sounds. Examples of long [a] sounds include b*a*ke and compl*ai*n, and examples of short [a] sounds include b*a*t and *a*ctor. As you will learn in this chapter, there are several other phonetic manifestations of [a]. In addition, we will learn about the various sounds found in words, the place and manner of the location in the mouth where these sounds are produced as well as the vibrational or voicing features of these sounds.

## Vowel Sounds in the English Language

### Singular Vowels

In English, singular vowels have a variety of sounds, which include short, long and schwa sounds. Notice how the same spelling manifest as different sounds in different words.

| | |
|---|---|
| iː | b*ee*; b*e*; k*ey*; b*ea*ch; bab*y*; bel*ie*ve; c*ei*ling; *e*ve; su*i*te; fur*i*ous |
| ɪ | g*i*ve; h*y*mn |
| ʊ | c*oo*k; p*u*sh |
| uː | f*oo*d; fl*u*ke; gr*ou*p; fl*ew*; gl*ue*; s*ui*t; sh*oe*; thr*ou*gh |
| e | f*e*d; br*ea*d |
| ɜː | h*er*; h*ea*rd; w*or*d; b*i*rd; t*u*rn |
| ə | d*o*zen; giv*e*n; fam*ou*s; fount*ai*n; pres*i*dent |

| ɔː | s*o*rt; bo*a*rd; fo*u*r; t*o*re |
| ʌ | h*u*t; fl*oo*d; t*ou*gh |
| ɑː | p*a*rt; he*a*rt |
| ɒ | *ough*t; c*a*lled; l*aw*; b*a*ll n*o*t; *Au*ckland; c*o*st |
| æ | s*a*t |

## Dipthongs

In English, there are eight dipthongs, or vowels that combine with other vowels to make a sound.

| ʊə | p*oo*r; t*ou*r; s*u*re; jan*ua*ry |
| ɔɪ | o*i*l; b*oy* |
| əʊ | g*o*; sl*ow* |
| eə | h*ai*r; w*ea*r; fl*a*re; the*re*; the*i*r |
| ɑɪ | fl*y*; dec*i*de; b*uy*; *I*; *eye*; p*ie*; s*igh*t; h*ei*ght, b*i*nd, w*i*ld |
| ɑʊ | f*ou*nd; *ow*l; *ou*t |
| ɪə | he*a*r; che*er* |
| eɪ | d*ay*; br*ai*d, gr*ea*t |

## Consonant Sounds in the English Language

### Singular Consonants

| p | *p*eace |
| b | *b*liss |
| t | *t*ruth |
| d | *d*ance |
| tʃ | *ch*oice |
| dʒ | ju*dge* |
| k | *k*ind |
| g | *g*ive |
| f | *f*riend |
| v | *v*ictory |
| θ | *th*ink |
| ð | *th*e |
| s | *s*mile |
| z | *z*oo |
| ʃ | *sh*are |
| ʒ | vi*s*ual |
| m | *m*other |
| n | *n*ice |

| | |
|---|---|
| ŋ | si*ng* |
| h | *h*eart |
| l | *l*isten |
| ɹ | *r*ead |
| w | *w*arm |
| j* | *y*es |

* Note that the /j/ phoneme is pronounced like the [y] sound in *yes* and not [j] sounds in ju*dge*.

## Digraphs

Like dipthongs in vowels, digraphs combine two consonant sounds. Some digraphs such as [ch] have multiple phonetic representations including /tʃ/, /ʃ/, /k/ or pronunciations. Some also can occur in various places within a word. For example, the diagraph [sh] can occur in any location within a word, whereas, the digraph [wh] can occur only in the beginning and middle of a word. The rules governing how strings of sounds can be put together in a word will be covered in more detail in the next chapter on Phonology.

| Spelling | Examples | Phonetic Representation |
|---|---|---|
| ch | *ch*ild, *ch*ur*ch* | tʃ |
| | *ch*ef, ma*ch*ine | ʃ |
| | *ch*aracter, an*ch*or | k |
| ph | *ph*onics, tro*ph*y, gra*ph* | f |
| sh | *sh*ow, fi*sh*ing hu*sh* | ʃ |
| th | *th*ink, wi*th* | θ |
| | *th*at, wi*th*out | ð |
| wh | *wh*y | w |
| ck | cra*ck*er, cra*ck* | k |
| tch | pi*tch*er, wa*tch* | tʃ |

## Place of Articulation, Manner of Articulation and Voice

There are three ways in which to describe each phonetic sound. The place of articulation describes the location in the mouth where the sound is generated. The manner of articulation describes how the sound is made using the formation of the mouth, the airflow and the tongue's formation and relationship to the roof of the mouth.

## Vowels

Vowels can be characterized by height, frontness, roundness and tenseness.

| | Front | | Central | | Back | | | |
|---|---|---|---|---|---|---|---|---|
| | tense | lax | Tense | lax | tense | lax | tense | lax |
| High | ɪː | ɪ | | | | | uː | ʊ |
| Mid | e | ɜː | | ə, ʌ | | | ɔː | ɒ |
| Low | | æ | | | | ɑː | | |
| | Unrounded | | | | | | Rounded | |

Pronounce the following words taking note of where the vowels occur in the mouth. A corresponding example word for each phonetic vowel symbol has been provided. Remember that spelling does not necessarily correlate with the pronunciation.

| | Front | | Central | | Back | |
|---|---|---|---|---|---|---|
| High | ɪː beet | ɪ bit | | | uː boot | ʊ book |
| Mid | e bet | ɜː bird | ə beaten | ʌ but | ɔː abort | ɒ bought |
| Low | | æ bat | | | | |
| | | | ɑː barter | | | |
| | Unrounded | | | | Rounded | |

## Vowels: Place of Articulation

The place of articulation for vowels can be described in terms of the height in which they are pronounced in the mouth and whether they are pronounced in the front, center or back of the mouth.

### Height

In terms of height, vowel sounds can either be pronounced in the high region, middle region, or lower region of the mouth. The sounds /ɪː/ in "beach," /ɪ/ in "give," /uː/ in "food" and /ʊ/ in "cook" are pronounced in the upper section of the mouth. The sounds /e/ in "fed," /ɜː/ in "her," /ə/ in "dozen," /ʌ/ in "hut," are pronounced in the mid height section of the mouth and the sounds /æ/ in "sat" and /ɒ/ "ought" are pronounced in the lower section of the mouth.

### Frontness

When you pronounce the front vowels /ɪː/ as in "beach", /ɪ/ as in "give," /e/ as in "fed", /ɜː/ as in "her and /æ/ as in "sat", you will find that all of these sounds are pronounced in the front of the mouth whereas, the sounds /uː/, /ʊ/, /ɒ/ are pronounced in the back of the mouth.

## Vowels: Manner of Articulation

Vowels are pronounced with the mouth open and lips spread or with the lips rounded. Vowels are also either tense, made through the tightening of the muscles in the mouth, or lax, where the muscles relax as the sounds are produced.

### Roundness

The sounds are considered rounded when our mouth forms a circle with our lips. Sounds that are closer to the [o] sounds are considered rounded. When we describe roundness for the sound /ɪː/, it is spread, where the sound is made through the whole mouth.

## Tenseness

Tense refers to the tightening of the mouth muscles. Take for example the contrasting sound in /ɪː/ and /ɪ/. When you pronounce the /ɪː/ sound in "be*a*ch" and /ɪ/ sound in "g*i*ve," you will notice that when you pronounce the /ɪː/ sound, the muscles are tensed. In contrast, when pronouncing the /ɪ/ sound in "g*i*ve," the muscles are more relaxed.

## Vowels: Voice

All vowels are voiced, or have a vibratory feature. The best way to differentiate voiced and unvoiced sounds is by feeling the vibrations in your throat. For example, if you pronounce the sound /f/, you will notice that there is no vibration. However, if you pronounce its contrasting sound /v/, you will notice a strong vibration in your throat. Contrasting sounds in terms of voicing will be covered further when we discuss consonants below.

## Consonants

Consonant sounds can also be described by the place and manner of articulation and voicing or vibrational force in the throat.

| | | Manner of Articulation | | | | | | | | |
|---|---|---|---|---|---|---|---|---|---|---|
| | | Obstruents | | | | | | Sonorants | | |
| | | | | | | | | | Approximants | |
| | | stop | | fricative | | affricate | | nasal | liquids | glides |
| | Voicing | - | + | - | + | - | + | + | + | + |
| Place of articulation | bilabial | p | b | | | | | m | | W |
| | labiodental | | | f | v | | | | | |
| | interdental | | | θ | ð | | | | | |
| | alveolar | t | d | s | z | | | n | l ɹ | |
| | post-alveolar | | | ʃ | ʒ | tʃ | dʒ | | | |
| | palatal | | | | | | | | | J |
| | velar | k | g | | | | | ŋ | | |
| | glottal | | | h | | | | | | |

## Consonants: Place of Articulation

There are eight locations or places in the mouth where these sounds are made. There are a few more places with some uncommon sounds that will not be covered in this book.

Bilabial        sounds pronounced between two lips
                sounds:  p  b   m   w

Labiodental     sounds pronounced between the bottom lip and the upper teeth
                sounds:  f    v

Interdental     sounds pronounced between teeth
                sounds:  θ   ð

Alveolar        sounds pronounced with the tip of the tongue touching or slightly touching the ridge directly behind the upper front teeth
                sounds:  t   d   n   ɹ   s   z   l

Postalveolar    sounds pronounced with the tip or blade of the tongue touching the area right behind the alveolar ridge in the palate or roof of the mouth
                sounds:  ʃ   ʒ   tʃ   dʒ

Palatal         sounds pronounced by the tongue gliding from the back roof or the soft palate of the mouth to the central area or the hard palate of the mouth.
                sound:   j (remember this is the y sound)

Velar          sounds pronounced in the back roof of the mouth using the soft palate of the tongue
                sounds:  k   g   ŋ

Glottal         sounds pronounced in the throat area with the larynx closing for a moment and then releasing
                sound: h

## Consonants: Manner of Articulation

There are seven ways or manners in which sounds are pronounced. The first three types of sounds (stops, fricatives, affricates) are called *obstruents* because there is a partial narrowing or obstruction of the vocal tract. The second three types (nasals, liquids, glides) are called *sonorants* because there is no obstruction in the air passage and the oral and nasal cavity remains open. Nasals and liquids are further categorized as *approximants* because they approximate both fricatives and vowels, where they create turbulence by the articulators coming close to one another, but not enough to obstruct airflow.

### Obstruents

| | |
|---|---|
| Stop | sounds pronounced by stopping airflow |
| | sounds:  p    b̥    t    d    k    g |
| Fricative | sounds pronounced with airflow continuing |
| | sounds:  f    v    θ    ð    s    z    ʃ    ʒ |
| | h |
| Affricate | sounds that are a combination of stops and fricatives |
| | sounds:  tʃ    dʒ |

### Sonorants

| | |
|---|---|
| Nasal | sounds which utilize the nasal passage and cannot be pronounced when nose is pinched |
| | sounds: m    n    ŋ |

### Approximants

| | |
|---|---|
| Liquids | sounds pronounced in the mouth, where tongue curves like a wave and the two sides of the tongue remain open |
| | sounds:   l (lateral)       ɹ (non-lateral) |
| Glides | sounds pronounced in the mouth where the sounds glide over the tongue and escape through the lips |
| | sounds:  w (bilabial)      j (velar) |

## Consonants: Voice

Another important way in which to describe sounds is through voicing. For example, for the sounds /p/ and /b/, we can say that they are both bilabial stops, but to differentiate these two sounds, we require the concept of voicing. If you put your hand on your throat and pronounce both sounds, you will notice that with /p/, there is no vibration in the throat whereas with /b/ there is a deep buzzing vibration in the throat. Sounds with vibration in the throat are called voiced sounds and without vibration, these sounds are considered to be voiceless sounds.

| voiceless sounds | p | t | tʃ | k | f | ʃ | s | θ | h |
|---|---|---|---|---|---|---|---|---|---|
| voiced sounds | b | d | dʒ | g | v | ʒ | z | ð | |

and all nasals, liquids, glides, and vowels

## Allophones

Certain sounds are aspirated, which means that there is a sudden burst of air when pronounced. For example, if we take the voiceless sound /p/ pronounced in /pʰin/ and /spin/ you will notice that if you put your hand in front of your mouth that in the first example, there is a burst of air when /p/ is pronounced as indicated by the /ʰ/, whereas in the second word following the /s/ sound, /p/ is unaspirated. In this case, both /pʰ/ and /p/ are allophones of the same phoneme /p/ because they occur in different environments where the aspirated/pʰ/ cannot occur after the /s/ sound where only the aspirated /p/can occur.

## Difference between spoken and written forms

In natural or fast speech in English, students often write what they hear in their natural environment. This may pose a problem in spelling particularly when sounds are silent in speech, but written when spelled or when sounds are added to words in fast speech, but do not appear in their written forms.

## Silent Sounds

English has some sounds within words that are silent when spoken at a normal speed, and are often confusing for English learners who write as they hear. Here are a few examples.

| | | | |
|---|---|---|---|
| wasn'(t) me | mus(t) be | you an(d) me | san(d)wich |
| int(e)rest | diff(e)rent | feb(r)uary | t(o)night |

## Intruding Sounds

Not only are there sounds that disappear or get eaten up as we speak, we also add sounds where they do not exist in written form. Here are some examples. In the second example below, remember, that the phonetic sound /j/ represents the [y] sound in yes.

The criteria [r]are stringent.    They [j]are hungry.       I want to [w]eat

In this chapter, we looked at the sounds in the English language that goes beyond the 26 letters in the alphabet. We learned about where in the mouth these sounds occur, how they are pronounced and the vibrational force that differentiates contrasting sounds. This knowledge of phonetics will help us to accurately address the pronunciation needs of our English learners.

## EXERCISES

### Exercise A

1. Why is it important to understand the phonetic chart? (Hint: Think about how many letters there are in the alphabet and how many sounds there are in the phonetic chart).

2. Write the following words using phonetic symbols.
   a. generous
   b. nothing
   c. scientist

3. In English, it is possible with the phonetic representation of spelling words for the word fish to be spelled "ghoti." Explain how fish can be spelled "ghoti" based on possible phonetic representations (Hint: Write out the phonetic representations of the following words: enough, women and attention).

### Exercise B

1. Find examples where these sounds are used in words for each place of articulation.
   a. bilabial
   b. labiodental
   c. interdental
   d. alveolar
   e. postalveolar
   f. palatal
   g. velar
   h. glottal

2. Find examples for each manner of articulation.
   a. stop
   b. nasal
   c. fricative
   d. affricate

e.  liquids
f.  glides

3.  Describe the following phonetic sounds in terms of their place and manner of articulation. The first one has been done for you.

a.  θ          voiceless interdental fricative
b.  ʒ          *voiced postalveolar fricative*
c.  ŋ          *voiced velar nasal*
d.  ʃ          *voiced palatal glide*
e.  ð          *voiced interdental fricative.*

## Exercise C

Describe the following vowels in terms of height, frontness, rounding and tense. The first one has been done for you.

a.  ɪ:         high, front, unrounded, tense

b.  æ

c.  e

d.  ʌ

e.  ʊ

f.  ə

## Exercise D

1. The symbol æ best represents the sound in which word?

   a.  card    b.  cat    c. kettle    d. heart

2. Which symbol represents the vowel in employ?

   a. ɔɪ      b. o      c. ɔ      d. eɪ

**Exercise E**

Identify an English learner who may need support in the area of phonetics. Interview the student or have the student introduce him or herself. Record the conversation (if permissible) and analyze the phonetic sounds your student appears to have some difficulty with and create two or three activities below to support the learning of these sounds.

Activity 1

    Sound identified:

    Description of activity:

Activity 2

    Sound identified:

    Description of activity:

Activity 3

    Sound identified:

    Description of activity

## CLASSROOM APPLICATION

### Kinesthetic and Visual Learning Styles for Articulation and Voicing

For the visible mouth areas such as bilabial, labiodental, interdental and alveolar sounds, you can show the students where these sounds occur and have them repeat these sounds. For example, English learners from Spanish speaking backgrounds may have trouble differentiating between /b/ and /v/ sounds. In this case, it is helpful to show them that /b/ is a bilabial sound that begins with the two lips closed and opens with a burst of air, which can be experienced by putting the hand in front of the mouth. For the /v/ sound show them how the bottom lip is touching the top teeth with airflow buzzing and flowing through. Students can also practice using a mirror at home to ensure the sounds are coming from approximately the same areas in the mouth. For the areas of the mouth that are not visible, use a picture of the mouth to describe where and how these sounds are generated.

In terms of helping students learn voicing features of sounds, have students put their hands on their throats and differentiate the contrasting sounds to understand the differences. Contrasting sounds are those that have the same place and manner of articulation, but are differentiated only by their voicing features. These include contrasting sounds such as /p/ and /b/, /t/ and /d/, /k/ and /g/, /s/ and /z/, /f/ and /v/, /θ/ and /ð/, /ʃ/ and /ʒ/ and /tʃ/ and /dʒ/.

### Phonetics Pictionary

Read words from minimal pair lists for your English learners based on their needs. For example, you may begin the drawing exercise by saying "Draw a ship." If students are having difficulties differentiating between /ʃ/ and /s/ sounds or with the short /ɪ/ and long sounds /ɪː/ sounds, they might draw a person sipping some coffee or drinking a sheep instead. For English learners from Japanese speaking backgrounds, they may have trouble differentiating with /l/ and /ɹ/ sounds. Ask them to write the word "right" next to the ship. If they write "light" instead, then you have data that demonstrates that they have difficulty with these two sounds, and you can design more minimal pair Pictionary activities to help them practice these sounds.

## Cloze Songs

You can select a song that students really enjoy and remove portions of words with sounds that students have difficulty differentiating and have the students fill in the blanks. For example, you can have the students listen to the song, "You are my sunshine," and give them a handout with the vowel sounds missing. Students will need to fill these in based on what they hear. The first line has been done for you. You can also use poetry for this exercise.

*You are my sunshine, my only sunshine.*

## Phonetic Card Game

Create a set of cards with sounds students have most difficulty with and a set of pictures representing words with those sounds.

| Differentiating Consonants | | Differentiating Vowels | |
|---|---|---|---|
| ʃ | - picture of ship | æ | - picture of bat |
| s | - picture of sip | ɪː | - picture of beet |
| z | - picture of zip | ɪ | - picture of bit |
| | | uː | - picture of boot |
| | | ɜː | - picture of bird |
| | | e | - picture of bet |
| | | ʌ | - picture of but |

There are several activities you can do with these cards. One activity would be to lay out the sounds on the table and have students pick out the sound for the picture you show. Another activity would be to have students show each other pictures and have their partners pick out the sounds on the table. A third activity would be to have you or your students say a word and have their partners pronounce the words or act them out.

# 4 PHONOLOGY

*Phonology* is the study of the rules that govern how sounds are strung together in a word. In every language there are certain rules that guide where a sequence of sounds can be produced within a word.

Take the word "psychology" for example. Though the word begins with a /p/, we do not pronounce the initial /p/ sound. Using the phonetic chart on page 19, the sounds in this word are represented in the following way: sɑɪkɑːlədʒi. In the English language, the phonemic sequence /ps/ can occur word medially as in the word "up*s*et" and in the word final position as in the word "sto*ps*," however, we do not hear this string of sounds in the word initial position as in the word "psychology." Note that I used the word "hear" instead of see because we are discussing phonetics and phonology, which are concerned only with sound, and not spelling.

Let's take another example. The phonemic sequence in the following string, /spr/, can occur in the word initial position as in the word "*spr*ing" and in the word medial position as in the word "hand*spr*ing," but cannot occur in the word final position. In other words, no word can end with the "spr" phonemic sequence. You may also hear many Indian and Spanish speakers add an "e" sound before /sp/ or /sk/ segments such as /espɪːk/ "speak" and /eskʊl/ "school." This is because their native languages do not allow these sequences to appear in the word initial positions.

Like this, phonology examines the way in which sounds are strung together in words and the limitations of where these sounds can occur within a word.

## Connected Speech

When people talk in normal speed, we often connect the words in our sentences. These often confuse our language learners. Let's take the following conversation.

A: dʒɪːt?          B: nəʊ, dʒuː?

Could you guess what A and B are saying? Try to say it faster and tease each sound apart. You will hear, "Did you eat?" followed by the response, "No, did you?" Often, our ear learners will have difficulty in spelling because they have primarily learned the language through listening. Their verbal skills are often usually better than their writing skills if listening and speaking were the primary ways in which they have learned the language. They will understand intended meanings much more quickly and be able to participate in conversations often more readily than eye learners who have primarily learned the language through reading and writing, and therefore, the speech that is encountered in real contexts, often fast, is more difficult to grasp.

Here are some additional examples of connected speech we often use.

| | |
|---|---|
| And | burgers *n'* fries |
| Can | She*c'n* speak Italian. |
| Of | A glass *o'* water. |
| Should have | You *shouldh've* told me. |
| Could have | You *couldh've* told me. |

## Minimal Pairs

Minimal pairs are words with sounds that can occur in the same phonemic environment, but create different meanings. For example, "bin" and "pin." Both /b/ and /p/ can occur before the phonemic sequence /in/ but mean different things. For English learners who have difficulty differentiating between these two sounds, it could lead to misunderstanding or miscommunication. It would be important to address this with your students using the voicing strategy by touching your throat and explaining the manner and place of articulation of these sounds. Another example would be "bye" [baɪ] and "pie" [paɪ]. Both /b/ and /p/ here again are minimal pairs and can occur in the same location, but note that their phonological representation of the second sound is the same though they are spelled differently, meaning they can occur in the same phonemic environment.

Here are some other examples of minimal pairs.

| | | |
|---|---|---|
| /ɪ/ and /ɪː/: | t*i*n | t*ee*n |
| /æ/ and /ʌ/: | c*a*t | c*u*t |
| /ʃ/ and /s/: | *sh*e | *s*ee |
| /n/ and /ŋ/: | thi*n* | thi*ng* |
| /m/ and /n/: | ma*m* | ma*n* |

In addition to understanding the sounds and their phonetic representations, phonology provides an understanding of where these sounds can occur within words and the possible miscommunication that can occur if English learners cannot differentiate certain sounds that occur in the same environment.

# EXERCISES

## Exercise A

Provide examples of words for the following phonemic sequences in their permissible locations. If they are not permissible in that location, leave it blank.

1. /nk/     _N/A_        _✓_        _✓_
             initial      medial      final

2. /sp/     _✓_          _✓_        _✓_
             initial      medial      final

3. /fr/     _✓_          _✓_        _N/A_
             initial      medial      final

4. /kv/     _N/A_        _N/A_       _N/A_
             initial      medial      final

## Exercise B

Translate the following connected speaking segments into words.

1. dʒlaɪk smɔːr?

2. ʃiː selz sɪː ʃelz baɪ ðe sɪːʃɔːr

## Exercise C

Identify an English learner who may need support in the area of phonology. Identify a list of terms that have multiple spellings for the same sound. Consider how you can support your students learning of these words.

## CLASSROOM APPLICATION

### Rubber Band Pronunciation Activity

Using a rubber band, you can help your students with pronunciation practice through visual means. For example, you can use a rubber band to demonstrate between long and short vowels. Hold the rubber band between your two index fingers and demonstrate to your student the short /ɪ/ and /ɪː/ sounds by holding it close for the short /ɪ/ sound and elongating the rubber band for the long /ɪː/ sound. Write down minimal pair sounds with short and long vowels and have the student pronounce these words using the rubber band.

### Minimal Pairs: What's your Number

Put numbers 0-9 on the board or on a piece of paper and include words with various minimal pair vowel sounds. Use minimal pair sounds that would be most useful for your English learners based on their particular needs.

| 1 | 2 | 3 |
|---|---|---|
| sɪt | sɪːt | sʊːt |
| sit | seat | soot |

| 4 | 5 | 6 |
|---|---|---|
| suːt | set | s3ːr |
| suit | set | sir |

| 7 | 8 | 9 |
|---|---|---|
| sɔːrt | sɑːrt | sɒt |
| sort | sart | sought |

| 0 |
|---|
| sæt |
| sat |

First, model and tell your students your school or office phone number by using the words. Have the students check to see if they are able to get the correct phone number. Next have the students pair up and tell each other their phone numbers or make one up if they wish and have them check to see if their listeners were able to hear the intended sounds. You may also choose to have them create mathematical equations for each other to solve.

## Tongue Twisters

Ask students to practice pronouncing the following tongue twisters. Select the ones that your students have difficulty with based on their first language background based on individual student needs.

1. She sells sea shells by the seashore. (s and ʃ differentiation)

2. The thirty-three thieves thought that they thrilled the throne throughout Thursday. (t, θ and ð differentiation)

3. Truly rural, truly rural, truly rural, ... (ɹ and l differentiation)

4. Betty Botter bought some butter but, said she, the butter's bitter.If I put it in my batter, it will make my batter bitter.But a bit of better butter will make my bitter batter better.So she bought some better butter, better than the bitter butter,put it in her bitter batter, made her bitter batter better.So 't was better Betty Botter bought some better butter. (/ɪ/ /a/ /e/ /ʌ/ /ɔ/) sound differentiation)

## Sound Bingo Game

Create bingo cards and put 24 words with sounds your students have difficulties with on the board. Have students put the words in any order in each box on their bingo cards. Make sure the words are related in place, manner of articulation or can occur in the same environment. You may choose to have students complete a straight line in any direction, an "X" or a full house. If you choose to have students complete a full house, you may want to select at least five more words, otherwise all of them will be winners at the same time. If students have difficulties with short and long vowel sounds such as /ɪ/ and /iː/, you may want to use numbers such as thirty, thirteen, forty, fourteen, fifty, fifteen, sixty, sixteen and so forth. If they have trouble with differentiating between the /ʃ/ and /s/ sounds you may want to include words such as ship, sip, sheep, seep, shoot, suit, shot and sought. If your students have difficulty differentiating between /b/ and /v/ sounds, you may want to include words such as ban, van, bent, vent, and best, vest. If your students have multiple needs across languages, which might be the case in most of your classrooms, you may want to create groups based on your student's first languages, provide lists based on their particular needs and have members in the groups take turns being the reader.

# 5 MORPHOLOGY

*Morphology* is the study of the meaning units, or morphemes, within a word. It looks at the study of the historical influences or etymology of words and their formation as well as how they "morph" into their various forms. Morphology also looks at the ability for new words to be created or coined, and based on the familiar morpheme units within these words, we are able to understand them as they develop.

A common area of study within morphology that is familiar to most students include prefixes (*un*-happy) and suffixes (careful-*ly*). Prefixes and suffixes contain meaning, but cannot stand alone. They are called *bound morphemes*. The parts of words that can stand alone are called *free morphemes*. In the examples above "happy" and "careful" are considered free, *lexical morphemes* because they carry meaning. Here is and example of a word diagram breaking down "unhappy" into its morphological units.

# Morphology

|  | **Free** |  | **Bound** |  |
|---|---|---|---|---|
| Lexical | Functional |  | Inflectional | Derivational |
| words | articles (a, an, the) |  | -s, -es, -est | i.e. un-, in- |
| with | prepositions |  | -er, -est | im-, -ly, |
| meaning | (from, in, on…) |  |  | - ness, -able |

Articles (a, an, the) and prepositions (i.e. from, in, on) are also considered free morphemes because they can stand alone, but their role is more supportive of the meaning of the sentence than bearing meaning in and of themselves. In this case, they would be considered free, *functional morphemes*.

Bound morphemes, are further broken down into *inflectional* and *derivational morphemes*. Inflectional morphemes do not change the basic meaning of the word being used. For example, the comparative and superlative forms of the word, "big" is bigg*er* and bigg*est* respectively. Adding these forms to the word "big" does not change the essence of the meaning. However, when we add prefixes and suffixes to words that change the meaning of those words, these affixes are referred to as derivational morphemes. For example, when the morpheme "un" is added to the word "happy," the meaning becomes the negation of "happy."

Another way in which derivational morphemes work is in the way in which they change the part of speech or the class of the root word. In the example above with the word "big," adding the comparative or superlative forms did not change the "adjective" category of this word. However, when we add "ly" to the word "careful" the word changes from an "adjective" category to an "adverb" category. Although it is helpful to understand the meaning of prefixes and suffixes to predict the meaning of other words, we must be careful as this might not always be the case such as in the following example, "womanize." The /-ize/ in "familiar+ize" means "to make" familiar, which is the case for most words ending in this suffix; however, womanize does not mean "to make" woman, but instead means to have affairs with many women.

## Etymology

*Etymology*, or the study of the origin of words is a branch within the field of morphology. Here, we see in the word etymology, the Greek word "etymon" meaning "historical form" and "logia" meaning "the study of." Examples of "logia" manifesting as "logy" are in many subject areas we see today such as "psychology" and "biology." The study of Latin root words are often important for learning content specific vocabulary primarily in the science, philosophical and medical fields.

## Compound Words

Morphology also looks at how words are combined to create *compound words*. For example, "homework" is a compound noun, which combines two words, "home" and "work." Other examples commonly used in education include desktop or laptop computers, mailroom, bookmark, classroom, notebook, blackboard, whiteboard and lunchroom.

## Blends

Some words are considered *blends* where two words are fused together to form another word such as "brunch," which blends "breakfast" and "lunch." Interestingly enough, we have not come up with an appetizing blend to capture the combination of lunch and dinner, which could be either "linner" or "dunch." However, there are many other blends that are commonly used, but their roots may not be as familiar. For example, "pixel" is actually a blend between "picture" and "element." "Cellophane" is a blend between "cellulose" and "diaphane." Other blends that can be easily teased apart include "smog," which is a blend between "smoke" and "fog," "spork," which is a utensil that operates as both a "spoon" and "fork" and in more colloquial language, we may hear the word, "chillax," which is a combination of the word "chill" and "relax."

## Clipping

Other words go through a process called *clipping* and is very common when students talk about their subjects in school such as "math" for "mathematics" or "bio" for "biology." Other common clipped words include "doc" for "doctor," "gas" for "gasoline," "plane" for "airplane," "ad" for "advertisement," "exam" for "examination" and "teen" for "teenager."

## Loan Words

Some other words are *loan words* or borrowed from another language. Many terms related to cuisine in English like "croissant," "burrito," "sushi," "couscous," "hummus" and "café" are loan words. Other words include "morale," "limousine," "gourmet," "ennui," "camouflage," "chateau" and "fiancé" are loan words from the French language. The words "albino," "bizarre," and "bravo" are example of loan words from the Spanish language.

**Multiple Morphological Processes**

Many words go through multiple morphological processes. For example, the word "delicatessen" is a loan word from the German language, but its clipped form, "deli" is more often heard. Likewise, the word "karaoke" has gone through multiple loaning processes. The word, "orchestra," pronounced as [əʊkesʊtɔːrɑː] was imported to Japan. Then the morpheme "kara" was added to it. "Kara" is a morpheme for "empty" in Japanese. A familiar word may be "karate" meaning "empty hand" where "te" means "hand." "Kara" was then added to the clipped form of orchestra [ɔːke] creating a new word, karaoke, and imported back again to the English language.

**Acronyms**

*Acronyms* are words that have been created through the use of the first letters in a series of lexical words. For example, B.A. is the acronym of Bachelor of Arts. SCUBA stands for Self-Contained Underwater Breathing Apparatus. ATM stands for "Automated Teller Machine." Because of the rise of the thumb generation and the increase in use of "texting" and "chatting" as a means for communication, we have also seen an increase in many acronyms, which are part of the larger Netlingo, such as BRB for "Be Right Back," LOL for "Laugh Out Loud" and BFN for "Bye For Now."

**Coinage**

Then, we have words that have been *coined,* which are created to describe or name a new object or phenomenon or named after people or places. In essence, these words have emerged to meet the changing needs of society. When the computer became mainstream, we saw the emergence of computer related terms such as "mouse" and "dongle" to allow for meaning to be exchanged related to the use of a computer. We also have the example of "google" when it first came out with a primary function of operating as a search engine for the world wide web. Then, we soon began to hear "googled" in the verb form, which means "to look something up."

Now, we have seen the development of "google docs," "google drive," and "google hangout" where "google" serves as an adjective. Likewise, with the emergence of social networking platforms such as "facebook," we see the verbs specifically related to actions that can be taken on "facebook" such as "poke," "friend," "unfriend,"and nouns such as "wall." These manifestations of new words or changing definitions of commonly used words in a novel context are words that have been "coined."

## Allomorphs

As in allophones discussed in the previous chapter, there are morphemes that cannot occur in the same environment such as past tense ending [-ed] and plural ending [-s]. These are called *allomorphs*. Let's take a look at the example of the bound morpheme [-ed] with the function of changing the tense of a regular verb to the past tense form.

| /ɪd/ | /t/ | /d/ |
|---|---|---|
| wanted | stopped | buzzed |
| needed | watched | bugged |
| started | worked | listened |
| visited | missed | played |

In the examples listed above, what is the rationale for the different sound manifestations for the past tense [-ed] ending? Native speakers who have unconsciously learned the language would be able to intuitively tell what sounds right and wrong when they hear the sounds pronounced, but for English learners, it would be helpful to understand and be able to explain why these sounds manifest differently in different contexts. In the first column, we see that the past tense [-ed] ending is pronounced as /ɪd/ after regular verbs ending in [t] and [d]. For the past tense [-ed] ending with the sounds /t/ and /d/, we can see when we analyze the last sounds in each word in both categories that the first set /p/, /tʃ/, /k/ and /s/ are all voiceless sounds whereas the second set /z/, /g/, /n/, /ɪː/ are all voiced sounds. Remember that nasal and vowel sounds are considered voiced sounds. Based on this analysis, we can begin to understand the rule governing the various allomorphic manifestations of the past tense [-ed] ending sound.

Rules governing past tense [-ed] ending:

1) For regular verbs ending in voiceless sounds, the past tense [-ed] ending is pronounced as /t/ except for regular past tense verbs ending in [t].

2) For regular verbs ending in voiced sounds, the past tense [-ed] ending is pronounced as /d/ except for regular past tense verbs ending in [d].

3) For regular verbs ending in [t] and [d], the past tense [-ed] ending is pronounced as /ɪd/.

Understanding morphological units within words can support English learners expand their vocabulary knowledge. Using morphological rules to understand pronunciation can also provide older language learners with tools to help them monitor their own language use.

## EXERCISES

### Exercise A

Break down the following words into their morphological units. If the unit is free, then indicate whether the free morpheme is lexical or functional. If the unit is bound, indicate whether it is inflectional or derivational. The first one has been done for you.

    1. Abolitionists = abolish (free, lexical) + tion (bound, derivational) + ist (bound, derivational) + s (bound inflectional)

    2. teacher

    3. prettier

    4. unbelievable

    5. reopened

    6. notebooks

### Exercise B

Analyze the following sentences by labeling the morphological parts in each word.

    1. Julia and Ken studied in the library

    2. The students in the linguistics class impressed the teachers in the learning and teaching program.

## Exercise C

Provide two examples of words derived from each of the following word formation processes. If you are going to be teaching a specialized academic content or specific English skills, provide examples from this area.

1. Borrowed or Loan Words:

2. Clipping:

3. Acronyms:

4. Blends:

5. Compounds:

6. Coinage:

## Exercise D

Provide a rule that governs the plural ending [-s]. Write at least four examples for each of the following allomorphs of plural [-s] ending. Make sure that each example ends with a different sound before the plural [-s] ending is added. One example for each has been provided for each.

|  | /s/ | /z/ | /ɪz/ |
|---|---|---|---|
| 1. | cats | leaves | dishes |
| 2. |  |  |  |
| 3. |  |  |  |
| 4. |  |  |  |
| 5. |  |  |  |

Rules governing plural [-s] ending.

1.

2.

3.

## Exercise E

Identify an English language learner who may need support in the area of morphology. Identify a list of terms that are important in your subject area or English language skill area. Consider the use of root words, suffixes, and prefixes to create word families that could support your student's acquisition of content area vocabulary.

List of Terms

List at least ten vocabulary terms specific to the area you will be teaching or are interested in teaching.

Vocabulary Instruction

Select at least three vocabulary terms that you can teach using prefix, suffix or root words. Create word maps or trees to support and expand student vocabulary using these morphological units.

# CLASSROOM APPLICATION

## Vocabulary Power through Word Families

Select a prefix or suffix in your subject area and create opportunities for your student to extend this learning of your subject area vocabulary to other contexts. For example, in math, you may choose the prefix "tri" meaning three as in the word "triangle". With this prefix, students can create a number of words that are used in daily contexts such as "tricycle," "trinity," "triple," "trisect" and "tripod." In science, you may select the suffix "tract." A variety of words in science and in other contexts end with this suffix such as "contract," "extract," "attract" and "detract."

Common Prefixes

| bi- | co- | dis- | in- | mis- |
| pre- | re- | sub- | un- | micro- |

Common Suffixes

| -ful | -less | -ly | -ness | -ment |
| -logy | -able | -tion | -ance | -ous |

## Allomorph Dictation

Dictation is one way in which to understand the differences between spoken and written language. Read a paragraph from a reader for your class and have the students write down what they hear. If you do not have a reader, you can make up a paragraph using words with the phonetic sounds your students have trouble differentiating. Notice that dictation can be used to understand and assess a variety of linguistic areas. Here, we use this activity for understanding and supporting student's morphological needs. For example, if they are having difficulty differentiating the past tense endings of words which have three allomorphs /t/, /d/ and /ɪd/, then you may want to construct a paragraph as in the following example.

> Malika *arrived* home from school in the afternoon. Malika's mother *glanced* at her watch and *bolted* down the stairs because it was time to prepare some tea and snacks for Malika, so she *descended* the stairs and went into the kitchen. The breeze was cold so she *closed* the windows. Malika forgot her keys and *noticed* the door was *locked*. She rang the doorbell and her mother quickly *opened* the door and let her in.

# 6 SYNTAX PART I

Noam Chomsky is most associated with the study of syntax with his seminal work, *Syntactic Structures*, published in 1957. *Syntax* is the study of the smaller components or units within phrases and sentences, and the rules that govern their placement. Children acquire these rules through massive input they receive from their environment since birth and are often able to create novel sentences through a process of creative construction within the first few years of their lives. What makes language magnificent is the unconscious internationalization of these rules by speakers within a linguistic community where new and interesting knowledge and meanings can be continuously exchanged. On the other hand, for speakers of a particular language, the fact that these rules are innate and have often been unconsciously learned, makes this a challenging area of language to teach. As teachers of the language, it would be important to bring these internalized rules to a conscious understanding, in other words develop metalinguistic awareness, in order to best support and explain these rules to our language learners.

## Lexical and Functional Word Classes

Words fall into categories or word classes, which are further subdivided into *lexical* and *functional* classes. The lexical or meaning-bearing category includes *nouns* (naming words i.e. desk), *verbs* (action words i.e. run), *adverbs* (describes verbs i.e. usually, fast) and *adjectives* (describing words i.e. beautiful). Each class of words have a function or behaviors that describe their personality. The functional class includes *prepositions* (location words i.e. under), *conjunctions* (connecting words i.e. and), *determiners* (*possessive nouns* (i.e. my, his, her) and *pronouns* (i.e. we, you, they), *indefinite pronouns* (i.e. few, some), and *articles* (a, an, the)), and *demonstratives* (this, that, these, those). In addition, the functional class includes *complementizers* and *auxiliary verbs*. Complementizers include subordinate *conjunctions* such as those that precede dependent clauses (whether, if, for, before, since, because), *relative pronouns* that introduce adjective clauses (who, whom, which, that, those) and *relative adverbs* (where, when, why) that introduce adverb clauses. Auxiliary verbs are helping verbs which include the *verb "to be"* in present (am, is, are), past (was, were), and past participle (been) forms. Auxiliary verbs also include the verb "to have" in present (have, has, haven't, hasn't) and past (had) forms. The verb "do" (do, does, did) and negative forms (don't doesn't, didn't) and the verb "will" both in present (will) and negative forms (won't) are also considered auxiliary verbs. In addition, *modals* are also considered auxiliary verbs which indicate some possibility, permission, or obligation such as can, could, may, might, must, will, would, shall, and should.

Let's take the word, desk, as an example. The noun, "desk" can take on a plural form, "desk<u>s</u>." The adjective, "big," however, cannot take on a plural form, as in "big<u>s</u>." Why is this the case? The personality of nouns, such as desk, can take on plural forms. Adjectives such as big, in the English language, cannot take on plural forms, just as nouns cannot take comparative (desk-*er**) and superlative (desk-*est**) forms. In Spanish, however, adjectives take on plural forms to agree with their nouns. If the nouns are pluralized "flor*es*," (flower*s*) in a sentence their describing adjectives are also pluralized "roja*s*" (red*s**), which is not acceptable in the English language. Like this, while languages might have nouns and adjectives, it is important to keep in mind that they may operate in different ways.

## Phrase Structure Rules

Phrase Structure Rules or PS rules are like law enforcement officers in terms of how we put phrases within our sentences together. When we do not follow the rules, it is considered a violation.

The larger constituents, or parts of sentences, above the word level are called phrases. These constituents include Noun Phrases (NP), Verb Phrases (VP), Adjective Phrases (AdjP), Prepositional Phrases (PP) and Adverbial Phrases (AdvP).

A sentence (S) is broken down into a noun phrase (NP) and a verb phrase (VP), which are then broken down into smaller constituent structures, or parts. The rules that govern the possible order of words in phrases and phrases within sentences are called *Phrase Structure Rules* (PS rules). Left-to-right ordering of constituents within phrases and sentences are governed by PS rules. For example, in the (NP) PS rule on the next page, if the (NP) has a determiner (Det), adjective phrase (AdjP) and prepositional phrase (PP) in addition to the noun (N), then it must follow the left-to-right ordering where the (Det) precedes the (AdjP), which precedes the (N) and the (N) is then followed by the (PP). Let's take the following (NP):

A       beautiful       house       on the hilltop…
[Det]    [AdjP]          [N]         [PP]

"A" is the determiner, "beautiful" is the adjective, "house" is the noun and "on the hilltop" is the prepositional phrase. At minimum, "house" is necessary in the (NP), but when additional constituents are added, they must follow the left-to-right ordering. In the following list of PS rules, constituents italicized are necessary constituents in the phrase or sentence. Those in parentheses are optional, but when included must follow the left-to-right sequence.

NP    -    (Det) (AdjP) *N* (PP)

PP    -    *P* (NP)

AdjP  -    (AdvP) *Adj*

AdvP  -    *Adv*

VP    -    *V* (AdvP) (NP) (PP) (S)

S     -    (S') *NP* (Aux) *VP*

S'    -    (Comp) *S*

As we see above, Noun Phrases (NP) at minimum need to include a noun, but if other constituents are within the noun phrase, they are required to occur in a particular order.

A Noun Phrase (NP) can include just a noun, such as "Toys" as in the example, "*Toys* are important imaginary tools for children." If a (Det) "the" is included, then it must appear before the (N) as in "*the* toys" when referring to specific toys as in the example, "*The* toys should be put back in the toy chest." If the (AdjP) "noisy" is to be inserted into the sentence, the rule requires it to follow the (Det), "the", and precede the (N), "toys" as in "the *noisy* toys." If we want to be more descriptive or specific, we may add a (PP) such as "in the yard." According to the phrase structure rules for (NP), we would insert this prepositional phrase after the determiner, adjective and noun as in "The noisy toys *in the backyard...*" Other languages have their own phrase structure rules. For example, in Spanish, the adjective follows the noun as in the title of the famous movie, "Casablanca" or house white.

Prepositional Phrases (PP) also follow a left-to-right order rule as we see above for (NP). A (PP) at minimum must include at least a preposition (P) as in the example, "Jeena came *in.*" Most prepositions, however, include an (NP) as in "from the store." In the case of prepositions such as "from," it is necessary to have the (NP) "the store."

Adjective Phrases (AdjP) must have at minimum an adjective as in the example, "She is *fast.*" If an adverb were to be included to describe how fast she is, then we would insert the adverb before the adjective as in "She is *extremely* fast."

Verb Phrases (VP) must include at least a verb as in "She *ate.*" Here, we have a (NP) with one pronoun, "She" followed by a (VP) with just one verb, "ate," the phrase can also have an (NP), (PP) and (AdvP).

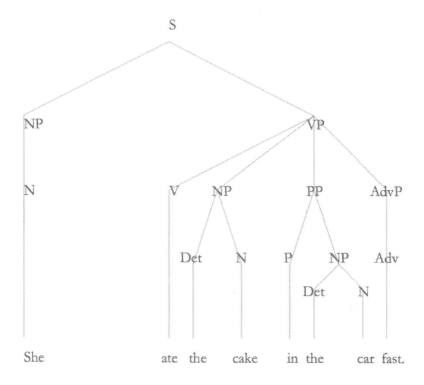

A sentence (S) at minimum must include an (NP) and (VP). In the sentence tree diagram above, the sentence includes the (NP) with one noun, "She" and the (VP), "ate the cake in the car fast." In the (VP), you can add an adverb phrase (AdvP) as in "She ate *fast*." Now, let's add another (NP), "*the cake*." In this case, the verb, "ate," must be followed by a (NP), "the cake" before the (AdvP) with the adverb, "fast" based on the left-to-right ordering of phrase structure rules. The (NP) can be further broken down into the (Det), "the," and the (N), "cake." If a (PP) were also to be included in the (VP), then, it would appear after the (V) and (NP), as in "She ate the cake *in the car*," and the adverb would follow the (PP) as in the following: "She ate the cake in the car *fast*." The (PP) can be further broken down into the (P), "in" and the (NP), "the car." The (NP) within this (PP) can be further broken down into (Det), "the," and (N), "car."

A sentence can also include a sub-sentence (S') with a complementizer (Comp) preceding the sentence and an auxiliary verb (Aux) between the (NP) and (VP). Let's analyze the following sentence.

When I go to the beach, Esmeralda will take the children to the park.

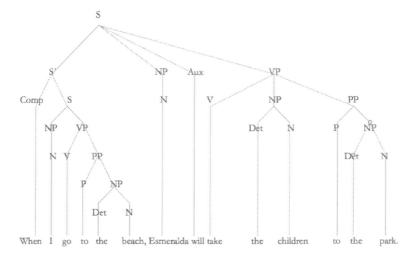

Notice that this sentence has a sub-sentence (S') or dependent clause, which cannot stand alone and an independent clause or sentence, which can stand alone (S). It begins with a complementizer, "when," followed by a sentence which includes the (NP), "I," followed by the (VP), "go to the beach." Within the (VP), we have the (V), "go," followed by a (PP), "to the beach." Breaking this further down, we have the (P), "to," followed by the (NP), "the beach," which can be broken down into the (Det), "the," and the (N), "beach."

Following the (S'), we have an (NP) with one noun or in this case a proper noun, "Esmeralda," followed by the auxiliary (Aux), "will," and the (VP), "take the children to the park." The (VP) can be broken down into the (V), "take," followed by the (NP), "the children," and the (PP), "to the park." The (NP) can be further broken down into the (Det), "the," and the (N), "children." The (PP) can further be broken down into the (P), "to," and the (NP), "the park." Here again, we can break down the (NP), "the park," into the (Det), "the," and the (N), "park."

## Deep Structure and Surface Structures

The deep structure of phrases and sentences follow the standard language order or phrase structure rules. Deep structure refers to the original version of the sentence before there are any movements. As you might have recognized, many of the phrases within sentences actually move around within the sentences. In the following example, the sentence follows the phrase structure rules. This statement is considered the deep or underlying structure.

> She was texting while driving.

However, this sentence can be transformed and can also be considered grammatically correct. This is known as the surface structure.

> While driving, she was texting.

We briefly covered dependent and independent clauses when we discussed Phrase Structure Rules as they pertain to sentences. Above the phrase level, we have clauses. *Independent clauses* can be independent or stand alone as the sentence in the above example, "She was texting." *Dependent clauses* on the other hand, require an independent clause and cannot stand alone as in the example above "While driving." Dependent clauses are like very needy boyfriends or girlfriends who cannot do anything without the other. In the sentence above, "While driving," cannot stand alone and requires the independent clause, "She was texting." What is important to note is that dependent clauses can move within a sentence, and can come before the independent clause as in the example above. However, these movements must follow certain transformational rules and are subject to various constraints – what they can and cannot do. These manifestations of sentences that transform from the deep structures through rules governing their movement are called surface structures.

## Transformational Rules: Wh-movement and I-movement

Sentences can transform from deep to surface structures as long as they follow certain rules.

When deep structure sentences become questions, they must follow two rules of movements: *Wh-movement* and *I-movement.*

Let's look at the following deep structure example and the transformation it needs to go through in order to become a question in its surface structure.

> Deep Structure: Marie is teaching English in China.

Surface Structure: What is Marie teaching in China?

When the deep structure transforms into a question in the surface structure, it needs to follow two movement rules. One is the Wh-movement and the second one is the I-Movement.

## Wh-movement

The Wh- (who, what, when, where, why, how) movement allows question words to move to the beginning of sentences. In this case "English" becomes "what" in its question form. So, "What" would first need to move to the initial position of the sentence. However, just moving this "wh-" word to the initial position, will make the sentence syntactically incorrect as follows: What Marie is teaching in China?

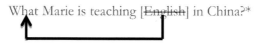

What Marie is teaching [English] in China?*

## I-movement

This question needs another movement to make it syntactically correct in its surface structure. The movement of the first verb in the sentence "is" into the position after the question word "What" is called the "I-(inflection) movement. With the I-movement, we now have a surface structure that is syntactically correct as follows: "What is Marie teaching in China?"

What is Marie [is] teaching [English] in China?

I-movement

Wh-movement

In addition to the movement rules, there are various constraints that govern movement within transformations from their deep to surface structures.

## Tensed S (subject) Constraint

*Tensed S (subject) constraint* is a constraint put on tensed verbs where they cannot be moved outside of their clause. Their role is to provide sense of time, state or quality of their subject and need to agree with the subject. *Untensed verbs* include verbs in their infinitive forms (to show), participle forms (adjectival verbs i.e. shown) and gerunds (nominal verbs i.e. showing). *Tensed verbs* include simple present and present progressive forms (shows, is shown, is showing, is being shown), present perfect and present perfect progressive forms (has shown, has been shown, has been showing), simple past and past progressive forms (showed, was shown, was showing, was being shown), past perfect and past perfect progressive forms (had shown, had been shown, had been showing), and modals (see definition on page 46).

Diego is expected [Diego] to come.

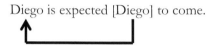

In this example, "Diego" is the subject of "to come" and can be moved to the sentence initial position of the sentence and still make sense because "to come" is the infinitive form and is untensed. However, when a modal "might" is inserted, we run into a problem.

Diego is expected [Diego] might come.*

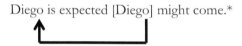

Remember that "might" is a modal auxiliary verb and therefore "might come" is a tensed verb. Because "might come" is tensed, the subject cannot move out of the subject position within the phrase to the sentence initial position. This is because the verb is tensed and requires its subject to remain next to it. This is an example of the Tensed S Constraint.

### Coordinate Structure Constraint

When we have two coordinated nouns (eg. salt and pepper; singing and dancing) in a sentence, we must keep them together in any transformations or movements we might make. Look at the following example.

Ramona likes to have [salt and pepper] in her bag when she goes out to eat.

Now take a look at the following example where the coordinated nouns are split.

Ramona likes to have [salt] in her bag [and pepper] when she goes out to eat.* Salt and pepper are part of a coordinate structure and cannot be split.

## Unit Movement Constraint

As in the example of coordinated structures in the previous section, phrases can be moved as a unit and cannot be separated. It is like ordering a lunch set rather than items a la carte off the menu. For example, the following sentence, [He [ate [a sundae] [at the bazaar]]]. can be changed with the prepositional phrase [at the bazaar] moving to the sentence initial position in the following way, [At the bazaar], [he [ate [a sundae]]]]." However, you cannot move parts of the prepositional phrase as in the following statement, [Bazaar, [he [ate a sundae] [at the _____]]]"* because the prepositional phrase [at the bazaar] is one unit or constituent. This rule is called the *unit movement constraint.*

## Subjacency Constraint

The *Subjacency Constraint* prohibits a movement of one unit or constituent beyond the sentence or (NP) boundary. Let's take a look at the following example.

[$_S$ The news [$_{Comp}$ that[$_{S'}$ a new book about spirituality was released]] was exciting.]

The main sentence (S) is "The news was exciting." Within this main sentence is the sub sentence (S') beginning with a (Comp) "that." The (PP) "about spirituality" can be moved outside the (NP) "a new book about spirituality" to the end of the (VP) within the sub sentence (S') as in the following example.

[$_S$ The news [$_{Comp}$ that [$_{S'}$ a new book was released] [about spirituality]]was exciting.]*

The Subjacency Constraint states that the constituent or (PP) "about spirituality" in this case, cannot move beyond the sub sentence (S') boundary of which it is a part as in the following example.

[The news [that a new book was released] was exciting [about spirituality]].*

In this chapter, we covered several important concepts in syntax that help us to understand the complexity of how language works. Syntax helps us to understand our incredible ability to create innumerable utterances, but within limits and restrictions. For native speakers of English, these rules become internalized unconsciously as they are exposed to their language over time. It is important for teachers working with English language learners to understand that these rules may differ from language to language and that the "intuitive" correctness of grammar or sentence structure is not often as apparent to their students from other language backgrounds as it is to them. Understanding how language works, particularly the rules that guide sentence formation, can contribute significantly in supporting their students from multilingual backgrounds raise consciousness of how English works, but also of how their own language or languages work. In the next chapter, we continue to explore additional concepts in syntax.

## EXERCISES

### Exercise A

1. What rule can you construct about categories that can take on plural forms?

   Example:          chairs                 beautifuls*

   Rule:

2. What evidence can you provide demonstrating that adjectives and articles behave differently and are indeed different categories? One difference has been provided. Think of two more reasons.

   a.   First evidence: Adjectives can take on comparative and superlative forms (small-er; small-est) whereas articles cannot (the-er*; the-est*).

   b.   Second evidence (Hint: review PS rules for adjectives and article placements within noun phrases):

   c.   Third evidence (Hint: think about the number of adjectives and articles that can be used within a noun phrase):

### Exercise B

Label the word classes (N, V, P, Det, Adj, Adv, Aux, Comp) and phrase constituents (NP, VP, AdjP, AdvP, PP) in each sentence. The first one has been done for you. You can choose either bracket or tree diagram representations.

   1. [s [NP[N Kailani]] [VP [V laughs]]].

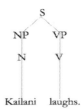

2. Mina danced under the stars.

3. Larry is sleeping on the sofa.

## Exercise C

Draw tree diagrams for the following phrases and sentences. The first one has been done for you.

1. the gorgeous view

2. from the patio

3. I enjoyed the gorgeous view from the patio.

## Exercise D

Explain why the following sentences or questions are not acceptable using violations of phrase structure rules, movements and constraints that govern transformations of deep structures to surface structures as explanations.

1. What Jessica will bring to the party?*

2. Thavam lives in Singapore in the house big.*

3. The roses are expected might grow.*

4. The farmers that grow rice in paddy fields in the countryside on hot summer days are resilient of Japan.*

# 7 SYNTAX PART II

In this chapter, we continue with the field of syntax. In particular, we look at the seven types or functions of phrases and the roles they play in sentences as well as how sentence ambiguity can be understood through syntactical analyses. We also look at word stress from the perspective of how it functions to change the part of speech of words. Lastly, we conclude this chapter with a discussion on the difference between descriptive and prescriptive grammar and how to approach each from a socio-culturally sensitive space.

## Seven Types of Functions of Phrases

We have seen that word classes have functions or behave in particular ways. Likewise, phrases also have various functions, which include *subject, verb, direct object, indirect object, subject complement, object complement* and *adverbial* or *adjunct phrase*. In sentences, we must have at least a subject and verb as in Kailani laughs. In this sentence, "Kailani" is the subject and "laughs" functions as the verb. Let's take a look at the following sentence.

Kailani gives her daughter lunch.

In the above sentence, "Kailani" is the subject and "gives" is the verb. The direct object of "gives" is "lunch." The way in which to determine the direct object is to ask the question "gives what?" The indirect object, or the receiver of the lunch in this case is "her daughter."

[Kailani] [gives] [her daughter] [lunch].<br>S      V       IO       DO

Let's take another example to understand subject complement. When the subject is equivalent to the predicate of the sentence, then we call the predicate the subject complement.

Her backyard was a haven.

In this example, "her backyard" is the subject, "was" is the verb and "a haven" is the subject complement because it is equivalent to the subject, which is "her backyard." In other words, in this sentence, "her backyard" = "a haven."

[Her backyard] [was] [a haven].
S              V       SC

The following is an example of an object complement, which describes the object.

Kailani named her dog Ipo.

The question you would ask is "Whom did she name?" The answer would be the direct object, "her dog." Ipo, however, is the name given to the "her dog" and therefore serves as the object complement, or equivalent to the object. In other words, "her dog" = "Ipo."

[Kailani] [named] [her dog] [Ipo].
S          V        DO        OC

Lastly, many sentences have parts that are really not essential, where the sentence can still make sense without these parts. It is almost like a hamburger without onions or tomatoes. The buns and burger are essential to the hamburger, but the rest are nice additions, though not absolutely compulsory. These nonessential components are called adverbials or adjunct phrases. On a side note, many faculty who are part-time employees are labeled as adjunct faculty. Though they are highly integral to institutions, this title often discredits their true value, so this title is continuing to be challenged. In sentences, adjunct phrases may be important information, but not necessary. Let's look at the following example.

Kailani gives Ipo dog food every hour.

In this example, "Kailani" is the subject, "gives" is the verb, "Ipo" is the indirect object, "food" is the direct object (remember "gives what?") and "every hour" is the adjunct phrase.

[Kailani] [gives] [Ipo] [food] [every hour].
S         V      IO    DO      Adv/Adj

## Sentence Ambiguity

Syntax also helps us to understand sentence ambiguity as in the following example.

Chika saw a person [with a telescope].

One interpretation could be to have [with a telescope] modify or describe Chika so that she saw a person while peering through a telescope. A second interpretation could be to have [with a telescope] modify a person where Chika, with her bare eyes saw a person who had a telescope. See the two interpretations based on the tree diagrams below. Constituent structures and the hierarchical structures or levels within the tree diagrams help us to understand the ambiguity in the sentence above.

Interpretation 1                    Interpretation 2

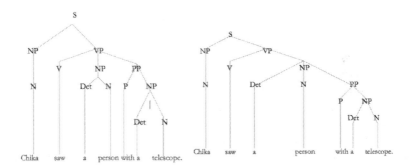

Notice that in Interpretation 1 where the (PP) is part of the (VP), this categorization signifies modifying or describing the action of the subject, Chika. In Interpretation 2, however, the (PP) is under the (NP) in the (VP) and hence modifies the (N) "person" within the (NP).

## Word Stress

Word stress is an important concept within several areas of linguistics. Word stress emphasizes particular syllables within a word. It is concerned with phonology and pronunciation, but also with morphology because it affects meaning of words. I have placed in this chapter because it also affects the parts of speech of words. For example, in the word "present," when we put stress on the first syllable as in "*pre*-sent," we mean gift or in the current moment or as opposed to absent. However, if we put stress on the second syllable as in "pre-*sent*," we mean to share something or introduce someone in a formal way. With the stress on the first syllable, the same word operates as a noun (I surprised her with a present when she came over) or adjective (Everyone is having a difficult time understanding these concepts, present company excluded, of course) whereas with the stress on the second syllable, it operates as a verb (I want to present flowers to my parents when I graduate). English language learners who may not have acquired or taken notice of word stress, may make errors, which can lead to communication failure. Therefore, it is important to teach word stress, particularly for words with multiple meanings based on stress being put on different syllables.

**Prescriptive and Descriptive Grammar**

It is important here to note the difference between *prescriptive* and *descriptive grammar*. There is a prescriptive study of grammar where there is a right and wrong way to use grammar. Imagine your grammar teacher with a ruler in hand correcting you when you say, "I ain't got no pencil." According to prescriptive grammar rules, this statement is considered ungrammatical because "do not have" requires a quantifier "a" for singular "pencil" or "any" for the plural form "pencils." However, this is perfectly correct grammar within the language structure of African American vernacular. In other words, in terms of descriptive grammar, what we hear in everyday language, this is common usage of the language. Like this, in music, movies and in our natural speaking environment, we encounter descriptive grammar. Like the African American vernacular, there are many Englishes that have developed over time within their own linguistic communities within English speaking communities and around the world often injecting their own native language structures and vocabulary into the English language. Some examples include Hawaiian Pidgin English and Indian English. Hawaiian Pidgin English developed in Hawai'i as sugar plantation farmers immigrated to Hawai'i to work in the fields. They came from a variety of backgrounds and mainly spoke Portuguese, Chinese, Filipino, and Japanese. In order to learn to communicate with each other, they developed Pidgin English, which is a mix of English and a variety of nuances and structures from these different language backgrounds. Indian

English originated during the times of British India, where the political and educational systems emerged with English as it primary means for communication.

The line between correct and incorrect grammar becomes fuzzy when we look at English as a Global Language developing within its own contextual and social communities. These Englishes are those that are an integral part of meaning-making for the children who grow up within these linguistic communities. When they come to school and are told that they are speaking "wrong" English, it is very detrimental to their historical and personal identities. Instead of approaching this from a deficit perspective, teachers should value the home languages of their students and the varieties of Englishes spoken and teach academic English as a second or school language, while allowing for opportunities for students to engage in their own variation of the English language or their native language perhaps during class discussions or group work where meanings are negotiated.

The study of syntax gives us the language to describe and categorize words and also to explain rules governing placements of these words within phrases, clauses and sentences. Teachers can use this knowledge to understand differences between the syntactical structures of their students' first languages and English and support their students' understanding and learning of the syntactic categories and rules when applied to the English language.

# EXERCISES

## Exercise A

Identify the syntactic functions for each phrase in the sentences below.

1. Kailani gives her dog a bone.

2. Her garage is a yoga room.

3. In the afternoon, Kailani makes her daughter flower leis.

4. Kailani serves lunch to the homeless every month.

## Exercise B

Provide an explanation for why the following phrase is ambiguous. You can use brackets or arrows to illustrate the ambiguity resulting in the two different interpretations of this phrase, or simply describe how this sentence can be interpreted in two ways.

British English teacher

## Exercise C

Respond to the following questions regarding word stress.

1. How does stress change the meaning and part of speech or word class of the following words?

   *re*bel:

   re*bel:*

   *per*fect:

   per*fect:*

2. What are some examples of other words with multiple stresses that may be challenging for your English learners?

3. What are some ways you can support your student's learning of word-level stress?

4. How would you approach the teaching of prescriptive grammar without devaluing the descriptive grammar used by your English learners?

## Exercise D

Identify an English language learner who may need support in the area of syntax. Ask the student to write a sentence or paragraph based on their proficiency level. Analyze this writing sample to see if there are sentences or phrases that may not be following English phrase structure rules. Consider ways in which you can help the student understand phrase structure rules without using the terminology, but rather visually through sentence diagrams, sentence strips, or any other activities.

If you cannot find a syntactical issue for your English learner, then use the following writing sample for your analysis.

"I live in the house of my brother. In our house big, I have a sofa blue.

My room is pink and I have a teddy bear yellow."

Activity 1

Syntactical Issue:

Description of Activity:

Activity 2

Syntactical Issue:

Description of Activity:

Activity 3

Syntactical Issue:

Description of Activity:

## CLASSROOM APPLICATION

### Identifying Word Classes with Color

Using student's own written work or a reading passage from a text, have students underline or highlight different word classes using different colors.

### Word Classes

| | | | |
|---|---|---|---|
| Verbs | - dark green | Auxiliary Verbs | - light green |
| Prepositions - | purple | Conjunctions | - pink |
| Articles | - orange | Nouns | - light blue |
| Pronouns - | dark blue | Proper nouns | - purple |

### Punctuation

| | | | |
|---|---|---|---|
| Periods | - red | Commas | - yellow |
| Questions | | | |
| Exclamation Points | | | |

### Sentences in an Envelope

Create sentence strips and cut them into their respective word classes or phrases you would like your students to study and put them in an envelope to be supplied to each group. Be sure to include punctuation in the envelopes that students can use to create their sentences. Have your students take out the sentences from their envelopes and time how quickly they can create sentences with words and phrases in the correct order. Be sure to take the time to review each sentence put together by the groups and highlight the different positionings between each sentence that makes them grammatically correct in their various forms. For example, for the following sentence, "I played in the park," students can also put together the string of words in the following way, "In the park, I played." Make sure that they place the appropriate punctuation in the correct position in the sentence.

### Student Sentences

In big poster size papers, include nouns, adjectives, articles, adverbs, prepositional phrases and other word class features and phrases based on your student's needs. Create a few pronunciation posters as well. Hand a poster with one of the above classes to each student. Ask one or two students to come up to the front of the class and hold up their poster with part of the sentence complete. Have other students volunteer to come up to complete the sentences with their respective word classes or phrases.

# 8 SEMANTICS

*Semantics* is the study of the meanings of individual words, phrases, and sentences. Within words, semantics is concerned with inherent meanings within words. For example, the word, "mother" implies a female and parent. In addition, it looks at the relationship of words to other words through the study of synonymy (words with similar or same meanings), polesemy (words with related meanings), homonymy (words which sound the same but have different meanings) and antonymy (words with opposite meanings). Collocations, which include words that occur together, also are part of the study of semantics. The categorization of words into hierarchical structures is also an area that semantics investigates. For example, a word such as "nature" is an umbrella term or superordinate term for "flowers," "trees," "birds" and "insects." These latter words that fall under the category of "nature" are called hyponyms. In addition, semantics analyzes the different thematic roles played by phrases in relationship to the verbs in the sentences.

Let's take a look at this puzzle and attempt to understand it from a semantic standpoint.

A father and son are riding in a car. They get into a car accident. The father dies and the son is rushed to the emergency room of a nearby hospital. The doctor comes in and says, "I can't operate on this boy. He is my son."

How could this be? If the father died, then how could another doctor claim that the boy could not be operated on because the boy was the doctor's son? The answer is that the doctor was his mother. The word "doctor" is often associated with the male gender; therefore, this scenario is one that still continues to puzzle many.

## Inherent Meanings

When looking at semantics within a word, we see that words have inherent meanings. For example, when we use the verb "kicked," the subject of the verb "kicked," implies a "foot" or "leg" that can engage in the act of "kicking." Therefore, we can say that the following sentence is semantically incorrect because of the inherent meaning in the verb "kick." Likewise, the word, "hand" is associated with touch.

He kicked me with his fingers*.

Instead, we would say, "He kicked me with his foot." Because "kick" implies foot, it is also not necessary to include the prepositional phrase (with his hand or with his foot) in this sentence. Every word includes semantic features.

|      | [animate] | [four-legged] | [concrete] | [wood] |
|------|-----------|---------------|------------|--------|
| dog  | +         | +             | +          | -      |
| desk | -         | +             | +          | +      |
| tree | +         | -             | +          | +      |

## Synonyms, Polysemes, Homonyms and Antonyms

Semantics is concerned with synonyms, polysemes, homonyms and antonyms. *Synonyms* are words with similar meanings such as "study," "investigate," "research" or "review." Semantics also looks at words with multiple meanings or *polysemes*. The semantic term for words with multiple meanings is polysemy. For example, the word "present" has multiple meanings. It can mean a gift, to be in the here and now, to share a piece of information such as in a presentation or to introduce someone or something. *Homonyms* are words that are spelled the same way, but mean different things. For example, the "bark" of a tree is different from the "bark" of a dog. It is important to note the difference between polysemes and homonyms here. Polysemes are related in meaning, for example, the word "bank" can be used as a noun to mean "a financial institution" or as a verb to mean "the act of depositing or withdrawing money from a bank." In this case, the noun and verb form of "bank" has two interrelated meanings that are associated with finance. Researchers who study semantics are also interested in how meanings may change over time such as in the case of the word "marriage," which has debatable meanings based on a religious, political or personal view you may hold.

*Antonyms* are quite complex and actually have three ways of describing them. Some antonyms such as hot and cold are considered *gradable antonyms* because they include intermediate levels such as "cool," "tepid," "warm," and "hot."

cold---- cool ---- tepid---- warm ---- hot

Next, we have *binary antonyms*, which are complementary and have only two categories and do not have intermediate stages. For example, a person is either "alive" or "dead." Semantically speaking, there is no intermediary state or phase. A third category of antonyms is called *converse antonyms*, which allow external states that are in neither category. For example, "husband-wife" is considered a converse antonym because one can be in neither category such as "engaged" or "single."

## Collocations

*Collocations* are groups of words that often occur together. For example, the phrase "fully aware" occurs quite frequently together based on the study of language patterns in corpus linguistics. We often hear "do my homework" or "run out of gas" used together. Likewise, when we read or hear about weight loss, we may hear "smaller portions" or "regular exercise" used together. A phrase quite often heard from a host after a presenter has completed a presentation may include the phrase, "...a round of applause." There are many such phrases when we discuss food as in the examples "bag of chips" or "loaf of bread." In the animal kingdom, we would group animals in the following way, "flock of birds," "pride of lions" and "school of fish." Learning collocations can support English learners to understand common phrases as chunks and participate in discourse without analyzing each component of these phrases each time, which can interfere with fluency.

## Superordination and Hyponymy

Semantics is also concerned with the hierarchical structures of words. The umbrella term or *superordinate* term that categorizes "apples" and "oranges" is "fruits."

Fruits {oranges, apples, pears, bananas, lemons, tomatoes}

Likewise "technology" would be a superordinate term for "iPad" and "internet." The sub-categories are called *hyponyms*. In the example above "iPad" would be a hyponym for its superordinate term, "technology.

Technology {television, iPad, iPhones, computers, radio, Internet}

## Reference

*Reference* is an important part of finding common ground in coming to a mutual understanding about concepts being discussed. There are four concepts within the study of reference, which is part of semantics. When we say, "That apple," we are referring to a specific apple. This is called a *referent* because there is a specific apple we are referring to in our conversation. Perhaps your roommate ate "the apple" you were saving for your lunch in the fridge, and she says, "Did you take the apple?" *Extension*, on the other hand, does not refer to a specific apple, but just a general concept of apple. For example, you may say to your child, "An apple a day keeps the doctor away." This reference to "apple" is a general reference. If a scientist were creating a new object for the market, he would have to create a *prototype* first, which would be an actual object that has the features of the intended object. *Stereotype* is a neutral term in the field of semantics used to describe a concept. For example, the following features "four legs, furry, barks" are considered stereotypes of a dog. These features are an abstract list that helps us to communicate our intended meaning if the term is nonexistent in our vocabulary or the word escapes us for a moment.

Reference also includes concepts describing relationships within and between expressions. For example, when two expressions refer to the same entity, this is called *co-reference* as in the sentence, "Gordon is our English professor." where Gordon refers to the English professor and vice-versa. When a linguistic expression refers to another person outside of the expression such as "She wants *him* to come," *him* is an *anaphora*. Reflexive nouns such as herself, himself, itself are usually considered anaphora because they refer to a subject mentioned earlier in the sentence or •

paragraph. For example, in the following sentence, "Joy takes good care of herself," the word, "herself" refers to the subject, Joy. When the referent is not obvious and takes into account the speaker's positionality, then it is called *deixis*. For example, if a mother says to her son, "Come here right now," we do not know where "here" is unless we know where the mother is located and where she might be pointing. In other words deixis depends on the speaker of the utterance.

## Truth

*Truth* is used to describe the truth value of sentences. Within sentences, we have *analytic*, *contradictory* and *synthetic* sentences. Analytic sentences are sentences with meanings of words. For example, "A chair is something you sit on." A sentence is contradictory when the words in the sentence make it false as in the example, "A chair is something you eat." Synthetic sentences require your presence to determine its truth-value. In other words, you need to see it to believe it. When someone tells you that they took an awesome class, the "awesomeness" of the class will require your experience to determine its truth-value.

In describing relationships between sentences and truth, it is helpful to understand the concepts of *entailment* and *presupposition*.

## Entailment

When the truth of the second statement follows the first statement then it is considered entailment. In this case, we only analyze the sentence and not the speaker's assumptions. The first sentence must be true in order for the second sentence to be true. Let's take a look at the following two examples.

Sheila got an A in Linguistics. Sheila passed the linguistics course.

In the above example, if Sheila got an A in Linguistics, then it is also true that she passed the course. We can say that Sheila getting an A in Linguistics entails that she passed the course. Now let's reverse the two sentences and see if it still holds true in all possible cases.

Sheila passed the linguistics course. Sheila got an A in Linguistics.

In this example, Sheila passing Linguistics course does not necessarily mean that she got an A because a passing grade is a C and above so we cannot say that in this example the first sentence entails the second.

## Presupposition

Presupposition is what the listener can assume based on the first statement. Let's look at the following two examples.

> Bobo took his wife to the movies.  Bobo is married.

In the sentence above, if Bobo has a wife to take to the movies, we can presuppose that he is married.

> Mojave likes the pizza from Mom and Pop's Italian Foods.  Mojave has eaten pizza from Mom and Pop's Italian Foods before.

Here, if Mojave likes the pizza from this Italian restaurant, then he must have eaten there before.  This is another example of presupposition.

## Thematic Roles

In a sentence, there are various roles that words or phrases play.  When English learners are able to identify and understand these roles, the meanings of what is being heard or read can become much clearer.  This knowledge is an additional schematic tool that learners can use to understand and negotiate meaning.  Gottlob Frege, a linguistic scholar, identified several thematic roles played by phrases in their relationship to a verb.  Generally, *thematic roles* include the following:

> Agent: initiates the action
> Patient: (animate only) receives the action
> Theme: (inanimate only) receives the action
> Cause: changes the state or condition
> Instrument: way in which action is performed
> Experiencer: (animate) experiences the action but does not control it
> Benefactive: benefits from action
> Goal: moves towards an end
> Source: where action begins
> Path: the route from source to goal
> Location: place of action
> Temporal: when action takes place

Let's look at the thematic roles in the following example.

The knight rode his horse through the woods overnight to reach the castle.

73

Here, "The knight" is the agent, "his horse" is the patient, "through the woods" is the path, "overnight" is temporal and "the castle" is the goal.

In this chapter, we covered some concepts in the field of semantics that help us to see the complexity of words and the meanings they carry. We looked for example, at the complex levels of understanding synonyms and antonyms. We also analyzed the categorization of words under their umbrella terms and the logic between sentences through analyzing truth value, reference, presupposition and entailment.

## EXERCISES

### Exercise A

In the following exercise, indicate the reason why these sentences are incorrect. Identify the words with semantic features that prevent them from being used in the following ways.

   1.   The rock jumped on this hand.*

   2.   I ate my computer.*

   3.   I kicked the ball with my hand.*

   4.   I smelled the wonderful aroma from the television.*

### Exercise B

How would you differentiate the two sets of nouns based on their semantic features?

Example
| heart, red, chocolates | vs. | monsters, witches, jack-o-lantern |
| [+Valentines Day] | | [+Halloween] |

1. table, chair, desk          vs.     water, juice, gasoline

2. table, chair, pencil        vs.     love, thought, idea

3. niece, daughter, sister     vs.     nun, woman, girl

4. steward, son, priest        vs.     ram, drake, bull

### Exercise C

Answer the following questions about word relationships.

   1.   Vehicle is a superordinate of which hyponyms?  List at least two

examples.

2. Pencils, pens, and erasers are hyponyms of which superordinate term?

3. If a *frunkle* is a type of *gris*, then _____.

 a. The word *frunkle* is a hyponym of *gris*.

 b. The word *frunkle* is a superordinate of *gris*.

 c. The word *gris* is a hyponym of *frunkle*.

 d. The word *gris* is a superordinate of *frunkle*.

 e. both (a) and (d)

4. Write two examples for each word.

 a. Synonyms:
 b. Polysemes:
 c. Homonyms:
 d. Collocations:

**Exercise D**

Circle the best description of the following antonyms: binary (B), gradable (G), or converse (C), and provide a rationale. (Hint: Remember that binary antonyms are pairs of antonyms with no other category, gradable antonyms have intermediary terms and converse antonyms are pairs that have potential for other categories.)

Example

 B G C   open        closed

Rationale: If a door or window is slightly open, it is still considered open.

 a. B G C   innocent     guilty

 Rationale:

 b. B G C   present      absent

Rationale:

c. B G C     hot                    cold

Rationale:

d. B G C     true                   false

Rationale:

e. B G C     married                unmarried

Rationale:

f. B G C     teacher                student

Rationale:

g. B G C     cheap                  expensive

Rationale:

## Exercise E

Circle the correct answer for the following in terms of concepts of reference and truth.

1.   The word *rose* and the word *flower* are related as follows:

      a.   *Rose* is a prototype of *flower*.
      b.   *Rose* is a stereotype of *flower*.
      c.   *Rose* is a hyponym of *flower*.
      d.   *Rose* and *flower* overlap.
      e.   None of the above.

2.   flies, chirps, wings, nests, has two feet, has feathers, generally small. This is a _____.

      a.   Prototype of bird
      b.   Stereotype of bird
      c.   Referent of bird
      d.   Extension of bird

3. Martha: It's the one on the right.     June: My right or yours? Why is Martha confused?
  a.   entailment
  b.   synonymy
  c.   deixis
  d.   none of the above

4. In the sentence *George gave me all her money,* *her* can be interpreted _____. (Hint: Here *her* refers to someone outside this sentence.)

  a.   anaphorically
  b.   prototypically
  c.   coreferentially
  d.   none of the above
  e.   (a) and (b) only

5. What kind of truth is illustrated in "My daughter's dorm room has two bathrooms."

  a.   analytic
  b.   contradictory
  c.   synthetic
  d.   none of the above

6. What kind of truth is illustrated in "A triangle has three angles."

  a.   analytic
  b.   contradictory
  c.   synthetic
  d.   none of the above

7. What is the relationship of the second sentence to the first statement?

  Suhar's son measures seven feet in height.  Suhar has a son.

  a.   entailment      b.  presupposition

8. What is the relationship of the second statement to the first statement?

  Everyone got a C or above.  Everyone in the class passed the quiz.

a. entailment     b. presupposition

9. What is the relationship of truth for the following two statements?

Victoria graduated from Harvard.  Victoria went to college.

a.   entailment      b. presupposition

**Exercise F**

Identify an English language learner who may need support in the area of semantics.  Develop a list of terms for your content area that could be beneficial to your student.  Consider ways in which you can help the student understand the semantic knowledge of these words taking into consideration word-level meanings, synonyms, antonyms, polysemes, and hyponyms.

List of terms
Write ten terms with important semantic concepts your English learners have trouble with or words you think could benefit them.

Activities
Select three words and develop activities to help your students learn these words.

Activity 1
    Semantic concept:

    Description of activity:


Activity 2
    Semantic concept:

    Description of activity:


Activity 3
    Semantic concept:

    Description of activity:

# CLASSROOM APPLICATION

## Words and Multiple Meanings Glossary

For any subject area, even for linguistics, it is helpful to generate a list of vocabulary words that are important for the content area. This list could include a word and its meaning within the subject area content, but here again, it is helpful to extend this out to other contexts in which these words can be used. The goal for teachers of English learners is not only to help scaffold their learning, but also maximize their learning, particularly when words and concepts can be used in other contexts.

Here are some common words with multiple meanings that cross content area boundaries. You can also have students draw images for each meaning of the words to support visual learning.

| | | | |
|---|---|---|---|
| present | plot | tense | value |
| figure | base | ruler | charge |
| bank | wave | bulb | class |

## Synonym and Antonyms Card Games

For this activity, you could select common words from your subject area or from a reading excerpt. In order to support student learning for these words, it would be helpful to include in the glossary as mentioned above, but also create some flashcards for students to test their knowledge of synonyms and antonyms. For words that are gradable such as (cold-tepid-warm-hot), students can group them in order of intensity. This activity can also be grouped with common prefixes from morphology that change words to their negative counterparts such as (non-, un-, dis).

# 9 PRAGMATICS

*Pragmatics* is the study of the situational context surrounding communication. Often, this is one of the most difficult areas for language learners to acquire because much of the meanings exchanged in conversation are beyond world-level or phrase-level meanings, but extends to a contextual understanding in which the discourse takes place. This contextual and social understanding of language use is developed as the participants are socialized into a particular linguistic community. English learners need to be invited and socialized into the linguistic community in which they seek membership, and explicit teaching of some of these concepts that are implicitly understood by those within the linguistic community, can be beneficial in helping them develop their sociolinguistic competence.

As such, one of the three areas covered within pragmatics includes *speech acts* or the various functions of language such as requesting or greeting. Second, it looks at *social contexts* within which the conversation takes place such as whether it takes place in a formal or informal setting and the roles of the participants in the conversation and third, the *discourse* or *conversational rules* that guide the conversation such as telling a story or opening and closing a conversation.

## Functions of Speech Acts

People communicate for various reasons. An analysis of speech acts looks at what is actually said or the *locutionary act* and the function of the utterance or *illocutionary act*. Locutionary acts could be *literal* or *nonliteral* as in the case of many idiomatic expressions. An example of a nonliteral locutionary act could be the following statement.

I am so tired, I could die.

In the statement above, the second part "I could die" is not expected to be taken literally, but merely means that the speaker is extremely exhausted. In this case, this expression would be considered a nonliteral locutionary act.

An utterance with an illocutionary force is usually marked by *perfomative verbs*, which are either *explicit* or *nonexplicit*. *Explicit* performative verbs have the force to create some change such as deny, forbid, ask, vow, and resign. However these explicit forms also have nonexplicit forms. For example, there is a difference in force between explicit performative verbs and their nonexplicit counterparts. Take the following example.

Explicit: He denied cheating on the exam.

Nonexplicit: He said he did not cheat on the exam.

Illocutionary acts could be *expressed* or *implied* or both. The expressed meaning is what is what is said in an utterance. In other words, it is overt. The covert meaning of an utterance is what is implied by the sentence. Let's take a look at the following example.

I forbid you to see that boy.

The expressed meaning of this utterance is that the speaker wants the listener to stop seeing a particular boy. The implied meaning of this utterance could be that the boy has done something unfavorable or has a quality that is not to the speaker's liking. It is subject to interpretation.

There are five ways in which to categorize illocutionary acts according to John Searle, a researcher in the field of linguistics. When an utterance is used to commit to the truth-value of something or some event in the past, it is called an *assertion*. Many news reports provide assertions when listing an event and the number of participants. When a speaker wants the hearer to do something, it is *directive*, whereby the speaker is requesting or ordering the listener to do something. When a speaker commits to doing something, the utterance fulfills a *commissive* function such as when the speaker promises or guarantees to call the next day. When the speaker shares his or her feelings, state or condition, the utterance is considered *expressive* where the speaker may welcome his or her guests or congratulate students on their accomplishments. When the speaker states a change of a condition or entity, this is called *declaration* such as when the president resigns from a company or when a priest declares a couple married as husband and wife.

Dell Hymes was the first researcher to analyze and break down communication into seven speech acts or functions. The most common reason for communication is *instrumental*, where we communicate to get our needs met. This is one of the primary reasons for communication, which begins quite early on. Remember in chapter one, we learned that children begin communicating by crying to have their needs or desires met. Another reason we communicate is *regulatory* or to control another's behavior. This definition overlaps with *directive illocutionary act* described previously. We often see children attempting to control their parents and of course, parents using language to control their children's behavior. A teacher may use language to be *informative* or communicate knowledge. A teacher may also use language for a *heuristic* purpose by working with students to investigate knowledge. Language is most often used for *interactional* purposes in order to maintain social relationships. Sometimes, a person may speak to express himself and his thoughts, opinions and ideas. When language is used in such a way to express one's individuality, it fulfills a *personal* function. This is similar to *expressive illocutionary force* described in a previous section. When we ask children or adolescents to think about what they want to be when they grow up or to think of other ways a story may end, they are using language to express a fantasy or for *imaginative* purposes.

Speech Acts can also be categorized in the following way. Language is used to *assert* (to convey information), *question* (to elicit information), *request* (to ask for something), *order* (to command action), *promise* (commit an action), and *threat* (unwillingly commit to an action). As stated in the section on "thematic roles," understanding the functions of language can also support English learners in understanding and negotiating intended meanings.

**Forms of Speech Acts**

Speech Acts can come in three forms: *declarative, interrogative* and *imperative*. Declarative sentences merely state information. Interrogative sentences ask questions and generally have a rising intonation at the end signified by a question mark in written form. We also have imperative sentences, which are "bossy" statements that you hear in the game "Simon says." In this game, the selected leader commands, "Simon says, jump on one foot." When the leader commands this, all participants must jump on one foot. Only when the leader begins these imperative commands with "Simon says," should the participants follow with the action. If the leader does not say "Simon says…" before the action as in "Turn around!" the participants would need to freeze and not do anything. Those who follow the command and turn around will be out of the game. All of the commands that the leader initiates such as "Put your hand on your head," "Clap your hands," "Sit on the ground" are all commands that fall under the category of imperatives. These are often used by parents to their children, the teacher to his or her students, really close friends and family members, but are considered impolite in contexts where there are participants with equal power who may not know each other very well. If used, this is considered quite impolite and may lead to pragmalinguistic failure.

## Directness and Indirectness

Another way in which to categorize statements is by understanding *directness* and *indirectness*. Directness is the literal transference of meaning. Indirectness on the other hand would be subject to interpretation or figurative. In many languages and cultures, directness is considered very impolite and indirectness is used to communicate requests and other such speech acts. Writing styles can also be marked by directness and indirectness based on the cultural background of the writers. For example, in academic writing contexts in institutions within the United States, it is very important to be direct through the use of thesis statements, arguments and evidence. In other cultures, it may be considered an insult to the reader to be so direct, but instead the writing style leads the reader through various arguments and perhaps may provide some insight at the end of the paper. Such differences are important for teachers to understand as they approach their work with their culturally and linguistically diverse students.

## Felicity Conditions

Within speech acts, pragmatics looks at the concept of *felicity conditions*. Felicity conditions are the ideal conditions that need to be met in order to deem an utterance valid or authentic. Within speech communities, often these conditions are violated through sarcasms, jokes or satires. Let us consider the example of a "question." When a person asks a *question*, there are three conditions that need to be met for the question to be authentic. One condition for the question is that the speaker does not know the answer and is therefore asking the question. Another condition that needs to be met is that the speaker wants to know the answer and has a desire to know the answer, otherwise, there is no point in asking the question. Lastly, the third condition is that the speaker thinks the receiver of the question knows the answer and is therefore asking the receiver the question. When a teacher asks a student a question to check his or her comprehension of the lesson just covered, the teacher already knows the answer so this is not an authentic question. More specifically, we can say that it violates the first and second felicity conditions for the act of questioning, where the teacher already knows the answer.

Let's take another example involving the speech act of making a *request*. When one makes a request, there are four conditions that need to be met. The first condition is that the speaker believes the action has not been taken. The second condition is that the speaker believes that the receiver of the request is able to carry out the action. The third condition is that the speaker also believes that the receiver of the request is willing to carry out the action and lastly, the fourth condition is that the speaker wants this action to be completed. There are many situations where felicity conditions around making requests may be violated. When we ask our roommate, "Can you please take out the trash?" or our children, "Can you please clean up your rooms?," the third felicity condition or the "willingness" factor on the part of the receiver of the request is often absent.

## Social Contexts

Another area examined in pragmatics is the social context in which participants communicate meaning through language. Researchers can analyze whether the setting is *informal* (i.e. playground, social functions) or *formal* (i.e. classroom, workplace) or if there is a power structure amongst participants based on age, gender, position and cultural background through an analysis of language tone, politeness features and word usage.

## Nonverbal Communication

In addition to verbal features that characterize social contexts, nonverbal features play quite a significant role in communicating meaning. It is believed that over 95% of communication is actually nonverbal. Gestures, facial expressions, eye contact, communicative distance and conceptions of time are all associated with nonverbal communication, but have a significant role in communicating meaning within a particular context. For example, pointing in one culture may be considered common practice, but may be perceived as rude in another culture. Likewise direct eye contact in one culture may be considered a sign of confidence, but may be perceived as being too forward or a form of challenge in another culture. Indirect eye contact may be considered a sign of humility in one culture, but avoidance or even disrespect in another. Understanding cultural norms when it comes to nonverbal behavior is quite important considering the weight it carries in exchanging intended meanings. Assuming the cultural lens of one culture in understanding another, could often lead to pragmalinguistic failure.

## Discourse or Conversational Rules

Pragmatics is also concerned about rules governing discourse or conversations. For example, a researcher interested in *conversational rules* may observe how conversations are started, sustained and closed in various contexts. They may find that telephone conversations have similar beginnings and endings across speakers and that academic discussions between a teacher and his or her students for a particular class may have patterns or scripts. In addition to analyzing scripts, a researcher interested in discourse rules may also look at which participant in the conversation, or interlocutor, is initiating, sustaining, and ending the conversation, and how participants take turns during the conversation. More specifically, a researcher studying this phenomenon may look at the kinds of signals the participants use to take turns such as raising the final sound of the word in their sentence, pausing for a moment or using some type of nonverbal behavior such as hand gestures to signal to the others that they are handing over their turn and making a suggestion for the next speaker or a raised eyebrow to indicate a request for clarification. This latter request for clarification can be nonverbal and verbal and is also known as conversational repair, or what participants do when they fail to understand each other.

## Maxims of Manner

There are four *maxims* that guide conversations called Gricean Conversational Maxims. Members within speech communities often violate these maxims to play with language. English language learners often have difficulty understanding the violations of these maxims because they take meaning at the surface level until they are slowly socialized into the implied and contextual meanings of discourse. There are four maxims including the maxim of quality, relation, quantity, and manner. The *maxim of quality* requires the statement to be truthful. The *maxim of relation* requires the statement to have relevance. The *maxim of quantity* is to provide only necessary information, not too much information or too little information. Lastly, the *maxim of manner* is related to how you communicate the message, which includes being concise, clear and sequential in organization.

For example, a statement such as "My cousin's house is a hotel," violates the maxim of quality as the cousin's house is not really a hotel, but is perhaps as nice or as clean as a hotel.  An example of a statement violating the maxim of relevance could be a response of, "I've been working all day" to the question, "Do you want to go out for a walk with me?"  Though we may understand the implication to be that the hearer of the message has been working all day and is too tired to go to the gym, when looked at this utterance from a response style solicited by the question, this statement does not seem to have immediate or direct relevance to the question.  When a mother asks her child, "How was school today?" and the child responds with "Good," it violates the maxim of quantity as the mother probably is expecting more from her child.  Finally, when an answer to a simple "yes" or "no" question such as "Are you hungry?" is long-winded as the following, "You know that I am always hungry and trying so hard to lose weight – why are you always asking me that question?  It is so hard being in my position with all my responsibilities and I haven't even had a chance to shop for food today," it is violating both the maxim of manner because of its length and the maxim of relation, or may not be relevant to the listener.  It is important to note that there are gender and stylistic differences within one culture of what is considered acceptable.

**Idioms**

An important area that is a component of pragmatics is *idioms*.  The English language is filled with idioms, which often makes communication difficult for learners of English who may understand the semantic meanings of the terms, but not the figurative or contextual meanings underlying these phrases.

Common idiomatic expressions used in the classroom and often misunderstood by learners include:

Piece of cake  Hold your horses  Be on the same page

Know the ropes  Hit the Books  Hang in there

**Sentence level stress**

Earlier in the book, we discussed word-level stress, which includes considerations of pronunciation, morphology and syntax.  I place sentence level stress in this chapter on pragmatics because the stress put on various words within a sentence changes the intended meaning of sentences.  Like idioms, these understood meanings that are grounded in sociocultural aspects of the language within the linguistic community are often the most difficult for language learners to acquire, however with conscious effort on the part of the teacher to make these culturally shared understanding more explicit for the students, they will have the opportunity to learn these subtle nuances. Take a look at the following examples.

1. *Shane* bought Kayoko flowers.

2. Shane *bought* Kayoko flowers.

3. Shane bought *Kayoko* flowers.

4. Shane bought Kayoko *flowers*.

In sentence 1, when the speaker emphasizes "Shane," it leaves the listener with the question about why Shane and not someone else bought her flowers. Perhaps the speaker has another person in mind that would be more likely to buy Kayoko flowers - someone who is Kayoko's boyfriend or someone who likes Kayoko, but does not expect Shane to buy flowers for Kayoko. In sentence 2, when the speaker emphasizes "bought," the speaker is surprised that Shane would buy flowers instead of picking them for free from someone's yard or giving her nothing – perhaps he has a reputation of being cheap or miserly. In Sentence 3, when the speaker emphasizes "Kayoko," the speaker is intending to communicate that there is someone else who is more likely to be the recipient of the flowers from Shane. Perhaps the speaker is aware that he is dating someone or likes someone, but Shane giving flowers to Kayoko is a new development or is unexpected. In sentence 4, we can begin to get a bit creative. If the word "flowers" is emphasized, this is because it is the least expected. Given the context, we may understand this statement better. Let's say that Shane and Kayoko have been dating for five years and are the happiest couple in the office. Shane asks his colleagues for advice on the most romantic restaurant in the area and also goes shopping for a new suit. His colleagues in the office suspect that he is planning to propose to Kayoko during this romantic evening. However, when they find out that he has given her "flowers," they are disappointed. They were expecting Shane to propose to Kayoko, and give her a ring, not flowers.

Pragmatics is one of the most difficult aspect for language learners as it encompasses not only the grammatical aspects of language, but also the social context in which these conversations take place, which is often influenced by the cultural norms in a particular linguistic community. It is often said that when a person is able to understand jokes in a second language, he or she is becoming quite close to becoming proficient in the language. By providing English learners tools through pragmatic knowledge, they can slowly become participating members of the linguistic community in which they are seeking membership.

## EXERCISES

### Exercise A

Think of examples where you use language to serve the following seven functions.

1. Instrumental:

2. Regulatory:

3. Informative:

4. Heuristic:

5. Interactional:

6. Personal:

7. Imaginative:

### Exercise B

Circle the correct descriptors for the following statements.

1. Give me the mustard!
   a. Assertion      b. Question      c. Request
   d. Order          e. Promise       f. Threat

2. Give me the mustard!
   a. Declarative   b. Interrogative   c. Imperative

3. Give me the mustard!
   a. Direct      b. Indirect

## Exercise C

Which of the four maxim/s of conversational rule/s is the following statement violating? Explain why the statements or responses to questions in the following examples violate a maxim or rule. You may wish to select more than one if applicable.

1. For neither anomalous nor bizarre individuals this book will totally and radically challenge your cerebral cortex.

    a. quality        b. relation        c. quantity        d. manner

    *Rationale:*

2. What time is it? Well, the paper's already come.

    a. quality        b. relation        c. quantity        d. manner

    *Rationale:*

3. What are you reading? A book.

    a. quality        b. relation        c. quantity        d. manner

    *Rationale:*

4. Let's stop and get something to eat. Okay, but not M-c-D-o-n-a-l-d-s.

    a. quality        b. relation        c. quantity        d. manner

    *Rationale:*

5. Reno's the capital of Nevada. Yeah, and London's the capital of New Jersey.

    a. quality        b. relation        c. quantity        d. manner

    *Rationale:*

## Exercise D

Which of the following felicity condition/s need to be met for making the following utterances authentic?

1. The policeman *warns* the skateboarder, "I will issue you a ticket the next time you ride on the hood of vehicles!"

   a. The policeman gives the warning for the future.

   b. The policeman believes the action is not good for the skateboarder.

   c. The policeman believes that the action being detrimental is not obvious to the skateboarder.

   d. The policeman wants to ensure that the skateboarder knows that if he skateboards on the hood of cars in the future it could hurt him and the vehicle, is against the law and can lead to issuance of a ticket.

   e. all of the above

2. Pat and Chris are having an argument in a restaurant, and Pat throws a glass of water on Chris's shirt. Chris responds with *Thanks a lot*. It is clear that this is not an authentic use of "thanking." What conditions need to be met for "thanking" to be authentic?

   a. The act for which one is thanked must be in the hearer's best interest.

   b. The act for which one is thanked must be a past act.

   c. The speaker must witness the act for which one is thanked.

   d. The act for which one is thanked must be in the speaker's best interest.

   e. Both (b) and (d)

## Exercise E

Indicate the locutionary or illocutionary force of the following scenarios and statements.

1. One evening, your mother comes home and sees that all the lights in the house have been turned on. In an attempt to get you to turn off some lights, she says, "What is this, Diwali (festival of lights)?"

2. To express agreement, a friend says, "How right you are!"

3. A teacher says to his student, "I suggest you spend more time on your homework."

4. A sign on the side of the road reads, "Construction ahead."

## Exercise F

Discuss each statement below using as many of the pragmatic concepts learned in this course.

1. Cheryl: "We're going to the YMCA for Caydan's 5th birthday party."
   Bill: "I better bring my earplugs."

   What does Bill really mean?

2. "I apologize for giving you a gift."

   What are some felicity conditions of "apologize" that are being violated here?

3. A 5-year-old boy declares, "I now pronounce you husband and wife."

Discuss the verb "declare" and the felicity conditions that you think need to be met for a declaration to have an effect.

4.    Don: "Do you have the time?"          Mike: "Yes!"

What maxim is Mike's response violating?

5.    "You can say that again!"

What is the implicit meaning behind this statement? How would someone normally respond to this statement?

## Exercise G

Listen to a conversation on television or in a public place such as a coffee shop. Take notes on the ways in which participants open the conversation, sustain the conversation and close the conversation.

1.    What phrases or gestures were used to open the conversation?

2.    What signals are used to indicate changes in speakers?

3.    What was the overall topic? Were there changes in the topic? How were those changes negotiated?

4.    What phrases or gestures were used to close the conversation?

## Exercise H

Identify an English language learner who may need support in the area of pragmatics, specifically idioms. Have the student keep a journal of all the idiomatic expressions they encounter in daily conversations and the television or radio. Design activities that can support his or her learning of these expressions.

Activity 1

    Idiomatic Expression:

    Description of Activity:

Activity 2

    Idiomatic Expression:

    Description of Activity:

Activity 3

    Idiomatic Expression:

    Description of Activity:

## CLASSROOM APPLICATION

### Idioms Jigsaw

Select examples of common idioms used in daily conversations in schools and in television and divide your class into teams. You can select the number of idiomatic expressions and teams depending on the number of students in your classroom. For example, if you have 16 students, then each team will have four members (Student A, Student B, Student C and Student D). You could choose four idioms for each home team to learn. Then, all of the students will meet with students from their other teams with the same letter. They will jigsaw teach their four idioms learned in their home teams to this group and will learn twelve additional idiomatic expressions from their peers (sixteen in total including the four idioms they learned in their home teams). They will then return to their original teams and create a story, conversation or role play including any number of idiomatic expressions. You may select ten or all sixteen expressions. If you have a class of 25 students, then you can have five teams with Students A through E and follow the activity in the same manner.

### Sentence-level Stress Role Play

Divide your class into four groups. Hand out the same sentence to each group, but with a different word stressed in each sentence. Ask the students to come up with role-plays or conversation scenarios that warrant stress on that particular word. You can use the following example or one that is from a poem, story or song you are currently using.

Group 1: The *teacher* gave the students a make-up exam.

Group 2: The teacher gave the *students* a make-up exam.

Group 3: The teacher gave the students a *make-up* exam.

Group 4: The teacher gave the students a make-up *exam*.

# 10 AFTERWORD

There are many reasons that have drawn me to the study of language and linguistics. In the following section, I share the role that language played within the history and experiences of my family.

My parent's native tongue is Sindhi, a Northwestern Indian language. Sindh was part of mainland India before the partition of Pakistan and India during World War II. After the partition, my father's family fled to the southwestern and central regions of India as did many Sindhis. In Sindh, he was in fifth grade with Sindhi as the medium of instruction; however, when he arrived in a school in the south central region of India, he was placed into a first grade classroom because he had no prior knowledge of Hindi and English, the languages used in the schools in India. He recalls this experience as trying and humiliating to say the least. At the age of 17, he moved to Hong Kong to work twelve-hour shifts in a relative's textile shop from 9 a.m. to 9 p.m., with only one day off a year for Chinese New Year's Day. He regularly sent money back home to his family as they had lost their family wealth during the partition. He spoke English to his customers daily, and learned Cantonese to communicate with his Chinese-speaking customers.

My mother was born in Sindh, but during the partition, she lived in Indonesia, where her father had a business. She lived in Indonesia for eight years and attended schools there. She picked up the Indonesian language through her interactions with her Indonesian friends and the community. When her family moved to India after the partition, they moved to a southern region of India, where Tamil was the regional language of the people. Like my father, my mother spoke Sindhi, her native tongue, Indonesian, the language of the land where she spent several years of her childhood, Tamil, the language of the people of the southern region she lived in in India, Hindi, the national language of India and English, the language of the schools set up during the time of British India.

My parents had an arranged marriage and soon after their wedding, my father moved back to Hong Kong to work and my mother remained in India until my father was ready to have my mother and my oldest sister join him. The Hong Kong market was saturated with Indians in the textile business, so when my father heard of opportunities in Japan, he decided to set up our family there instead. After a few years, he called my mother to come to settle in Japan. When my mother arrived with my sister, who was four years old at that time, she was so afraid of this new country and its people, that she pulled down all the shutters in the house for three full days and did not step out. My middle sister and I were born in this small village in Japan.

My father found two other Indian families in the neighborhood in Japan who were Punjabis, people from a region in Northern India. My mother learned conversational Punjabi from her interactions with them. She slowly adjusted to life in Japan, picked up Japanese and found a small, but steadily growing Indian community about an hour away in Kobe.

My mother would attend Bollywood movie nights, cultural and spiritual events and slowly became integrated into the Indian community within the Japanese community. She became part of the Japanese hiking community and learned to speak Japanese through her daily interactions with them as well as through meeting her daily needs of running a household such as shopping, speaking on the telephone, banking and ordering food at a restaurant. She preserved her Sindhi language through engaging in Sindhi community events and moving to a street within Kobe, in an apartment owned and lived in by a Sindhi tycoon.

My father worked in an import and export textile company and learned Japanese through bilingual phrase books, television, and through daily conducting of business exchanges. My father travelled for three months at a time on business trips to secure orders from international markets for orders to be manufactured in Japan. He would export textiles in containers to international markets all over the world. These countries included countries in Asia (Hong Kong, Singapore, Malaysia, Indonesia, Nepal, India, Burma, Sri Lanka), the Middle East (Dubai, Kuwait, Saudi Arabia, Bahrain, Doha, Jordan, Iraq), Europe (Germany, France, England, Ireland, Switzerland, Spain and the Canary Islands), Africa (Egypt, Nigeria, Benin, Ivory Coast, Monrovia, Doula, Zimbabwe, Sudan, Kenya, South Africa), Mauritius, Australia, Fiji islands, and New Zealand. The language he used to communicate with his clients was English and was exposed to English in all the varieties you can imagine.

Two other Indian communities, the Gujuratis and Punjabis, lived in Kobe within a half hour of each other and had their own temples and community clubs. The Indians all interacted in Hindi or English and when general events occurred, such as Indian new years day (Diwali) and community organized events such as the Kobe parade, these communities would get together and take turns selecting one Indian representative from each community each year to represent India in the parade.

When I was four, I attended a Japanese pre-school in the neighborhood and learned Japanese through my interactions with the Japanese children and teachers there as well as from the television. There were two private English-medium international schools within an hour from these Indian communities where the Indian children went to school. I attended a Catholic school in Suma, about a 45-minute trip by bus and train each way when I turned five. Teachers in this school spoke a variety of Englishes including American English, British English, Irish English, Russian English, Korean English, Chinese English, Japanese English, Filipino English and Indian English. And within each of these varieties of Englishes, there were a full spectrum of accents. For example, I learned early on that there was no standard American accent because I had teachers from New York, New Jersey, California, and some of the southern states. Through these experiences, I was able to tune my ears to focus on meaning and understand messages in English regardless of accent. Likewise, I had classmates who were from around the world and English was our primary mode of communication.

When I would go over to their homes, I would hear French and my name said in a French accent, which I found funny at first, but came to love. When I would attend birthday parties, I would hear a variety of different languages, even Indian languages that I did not understand, but my ears tuned into these sounds and I began to be able to recognize these different languages.

I quickly picked up proficiency in academic English, through my years of schooling and casual conversational skills through interactions with friends and the slow, but steady emergence of American television, often shown at two or three in the morning. Although our schools provided rich experiences for learning English and understanding the different varieties of Englishes spoken around the world, it was often to the detriment of maintaining my home language and learning some of the other languages spoken by my peers. At our school, we were forbidden to speak Japanese or any of our home languages. If you did speak Japanese or our home language and were caught, you were given a detention slip. Such policies had adverse consequences for not only my sense of identity and the ability to express myself, but also for my potential to become fully multilingual.

In my community, we spoke in English when we communicated with one another, interacted in Japanese when we left our small Indian community and engaged in activities in the expanded Japanese community. At home, my parents also emphasized the importance of speaking English and discouraged me from speaking my native tongue, Sindhi. Because they spoke this language to one another and to us on many occasions, I am still able to understand much of what is being said, but am not fluent in my speaking ability. Another lost opportunity. Of course with India's booming movie industry, I picked up listening proficiency in Hindi, but with a lack of opportunity to speak it, I have not been able to develop my speaking proficiency in this language.

I began teaching English at the age of 16. Since then, I have gained formal training in the theories and methodologies of teaching English and have taught in a multitude of different environments to students of various English proficiency levels and language backgrounds. From these experiences, I have come to understand the complex teaching demands of teachers working in multilingual and multi-cultural classrooms. This has now become our new "normal." In light of the expanding role of English on the global platform, the methodology of teaching "correct" grammar or what comprises "native accent" is slowly being shifted into a new paradigm, which honors the various Englishes that have evolved in different parts of the world and linguistic communities within English speaking countries as well. These Englishes have served these communities in communicating across language and cultural boundaries. It has provided a space for intercultural learning, business and educational opportunities and international friendships.

Today, teachers have an incredible opportunity to support the development of their students' academic and language proficiencies so that they, too can have the ability to engage on the global platform.

# EXERCISES

## Exercise A

Answer the following questions about the afterword.

1. What is your history with language?

2. How has your understanding of English changed after reading the afterword?

3. How can you approach developing your student's English proficiency from a global perspective?

## Exercise B

Answer the following questions about your learning from this book.

1. How might your approach to working with students from multilingual backgrounds be supported through the understanding of linguistics you gained from this book?

2. What are some activities you think will be helpful in supporting your future student's needs in the area of linguistics?

# CLASSROOM APPLICATION

## Final Case Study Project

Throughout these chapters, you practiced some of linguistic activities to support your English learner's needs in each of the six areas of linguistics. For this final case study project, conduct a comprehensive analysis of one English learner's first language background and English through interviews with the student and his or her teacher, reviewing of student written and spoken samples or artifacts and conducting research of the student's first language. Identify possible issues in each of the areas of linguistics studied in this book. Develop activities for each area and try them out with your student. Reflect on your student's learning of the concepts in each area. Think about next steps and how you can better support their needs in the future. In the following pages, a mini-lesson plan for each area of linguistics has been provided.

| Linguistic Area | Phonetics |
|---|---|
| Linguistic Issue | |
| Activity | |
| Student Learning<br><br>How did your student do? | |
| Reflections<br><br>How did the lesson go?<br>How do you know?<br>In what area does your student need more support? | |

| | |
|---|---|
| **Linguistic Area** | Phonology |
| **Linguistic Issue** | |
| **Activity** | |
| **Student Learning**<br><br>How did your student do? | |
| **Reflections**<br><br>How did the lesson go?<br>How do you know?<br>In what area does your student need more support? | |

Additional Notes:

| Linguistic Area | Morphology |
| --- | --- |
| **Linguistic Issue** | |
| **Activity** | |
| **Student Learning**<br><br>How did your student do? | |
| **Reflections**<br><br>How did the lesson go?<br>How do you know?<br>In what area does your student need more support? | |

Additional Notes:

| | |
|---|---|
| **Linguistic Area** | Syntax |
| **Linguistic Issue** | |
| **Activity** | |
| **Student Learning**<br><br>How did your student do? | |
| **Reflections**<br><br>How did the lesson go?<br>How do you know?<br>In what area does your student need more support? | |

Additional Notes:

| | |
|---|---|
| **Linguistic Area** | Semantics |
| **Linguistic Issue** | |
| **Activity** | |
| **Student Learning**<br><br>How did your student do? | |
| **Reflections**<br><br>How did the lesson go?<br>How do you know?<br>In what area does your student need<br>more support? | |

Additional Notes:

| | |
|---|---|
| **Linguistic Area** | Pragmatics |
| **Linguistic Issue** | |
| **Activity** | |
| **Student Learning**<br><br>How did your student do? | |
| **Reflections**<br><br>How did the lesson go?<br>How do you know?<br>In what area does your student need more support? | |

Additional Notes

# REFERENCES

Barry, A. K. (2002). *Linguistic perspectives on language and education.* Westport, CT: Bergin & Garvey.

Chomsky, Noam (1957). *Syntactic structures.* London, UK: Mouton.

Corder, S.P. (1967). The significance of learners' errors. *IRAL,* 5, 161-170.

Darling-Hammond, L. (1997). Forward. In J. E. King, E. R. Hollins & W. C. Hayman, (Eds.), *Preparing teachers for cultural diversity* (pp. i-4). New York, NY: Teachers College Press.

Freeman, D. E. & Freeman, Y. S. (2004). *Essential linguistics: What you need to know to teach reading, ESL, spelling, phonics and grammar.* Portsmouth, NH: Heinemann.

Fromkin, V. A. (2002). *Linguistics: An Introduction to Linguistic Theory.* Hoboken, NJ: Blackwell Publishers.

Grice, H.P. (1975). Logic and Conversation. In: P. Cole and J.L. Morgan (eds.), *Syntax and Semantics 3: Speech Acts,* 41-58. New York: Academic Press.

Harley, H. (2010). Thematic roles. In P. Hogan (Ed.), *The Cambridge Encyclopedia of the Language Sciences* (pp. 861-862). Cambridge, MA: Cambridge University Press,

Hudson, G. (2000). *Essential introductory linguistics.* Malden, MA: Blackwell Publishing.

Krashen, S. (1982). *Principles and practice in second language acquisition.* Oxford, UK: Pergamon Press, Inc.

OGrady, W., Archibald, J., Aronoff, M. and Rees-Miller, J. (2001). *Contemporary Linguistics,* 4th edition. Boston, MA: St. Martin's Press.

Parker, F. & Riley, K. (2004). Phonology. In *Linguistics for non-Linguistics: A primer with exercises* (4ᵗʰ ed., pp. 105-127). Boston, MA: Allyn & Bacon.

Parker, F. & Riley, K. (2004). Pragmatics. In *Linguistics for non-Linguistics: A primer with exercises* (4ᵗʰ ed., pp. 9-26). Boston, MA: Allyn & Bacon.

Parker, F. & Riley, K. (2004). Semantics. In *Linguistics for non-Linguistics: A primer with exercises* (4ᵗʰ ed., pp. 31-49). Boston, MA: Allyn & Bacon.

Parker, F. & Riley, K. (2004). Syntax. In *Linguistics for non-Linguistics: A primer with exercises* (4ᵗʰ ed., pp. 53-78). Boston, MA: Allyn & Bacon.

Schmidt, R. (1990). The role of consciousness in second language learning. *Applied Linguistics, 11*, 129-158.

Searle, J. & Vanderveken, D. (1985). *Foundations of illocutionary logic.* Cambridge, UK: Cambridge University Press.

Skinner, B. F. (1938). *The behavior of organisms: An experimental analysis.* New York: Appleton-Century.

Swain, M. (1976). *Five years of primary French immersion: Annual reports of the bilingual education project to the Carleton board of education and the Ottawa board of education up to 1975.* Ontario, Canada: Ontario Institute for Studies in Education

Tserdanelis, G. & Wong, W. Y. P. (Eds.). (2004). *Language files* (9ᵗʰ ed.). Columbus, OH: The Ohio State University Press.

Vanderweide, T., Rees-Miller, J., and Aronoff, M. (2002). *Study Guide for Contemporary Linguistics.* Boston, MA: St. Martin's Press.

Vygotsky, L. S. (1978). *Mind in society.* Cambridge, MA: Harvard University Press.

West, S. L. *Linguistics for educators: A practical guide* (2ⁿᵈ ed.) Richmond, CA: International Institute of Language and Culture.

Yule, G. (2006). Morphology. In *The Study of Language* (3ʳᵈ ed., pp. 62-67). Cambridge, UK: Cambridge University Press.

Yule, G. (2006). Word and word-formation processes. In *The Study of Language* (3$^{rd}$, ed., pp. 52-61). Cambridge, UK: Cambridge University Press.

# GLOSSARY OF TERMS

Acronyms:

Adjectives:

Adjectival or Adjective Phrase:

Adjunct Phrase:

Adverbs:

Adverbial or Adverb Phrase:

Affective Filter Hypothesis:

Affricates:

Allomorphs:

Allophones:

Alveolar Sounds:

Analytic Truth:

Anaphora:

Antonyms:

Approximants:

Articles:

Aspiration:

Auxiliary Verbs:

B. F. Skinner:

Behavioral Psychology:

Bilabial Sounds:

Binary Antonyms:

Blends:

Bound Morphemes:

Classical Conditioning:

Clipping:

Coinage:

Collocation:

Comparative Form:

Complementizers:

Compound Words:

Conceptual Image:

Conjunctions:

Connected Speech:

Consonants:

Contradictory Truth:

Contrasting Sounds:

Conversational Maxims:

Converse Antonyms:

Coordinated nouns:

Coordinate Structure Constraint:

Co-reference:

Declarative Speech Act:

Deep Structure:

Deixis:

Dell Hymes:

Demonstratives:

Dependent Clause:

Descriptive Grammar:

Determiners:

Derivational Morphemes:

Digraphs:

Dipthongs:

Directness:

Direct Object:

Discourse/Conversational Rules:

Entailment:

Etymology:

Explicit Illocutionary Force:

Expressed Illocutionary Act:

Extension:

Felicity Conditions:

First Language Acquisition:

Formal Social Context:

Free Morphemes:

Fricatives:

Functional Morphemes:

Functional Word Class:

Glides:

Glottal Sounds:

Gottlob Frege:

Gradable Antonyms:

Homonyms:

Hyponyms:

Idioms:

Illocutionary Force:

Imperative Speech Act:

Implied Illocutionary Act:

Indefinite Pronouns:

Independent Clause:

Indirectness:

Indirect Object:

Inflectional Morphemes:

I (Inflectional) Movement:

Informal Social Context:

Input Hypothesis:

Interdental Sounds:

Interrogative Speech Acts:

Intruding Sounds:

John Searle:

Labiodental Sounds:

Language:

Language Acquisition Device:

Language Learning:

Language Acquisition:

Lev Vygotsky:

Lexical Morphemes:

Lexical Word Class:

Linguistics:

Literal locutionary act:

Liquids:

Loan Words:

Locutionary Force:

Manner of Articulation:

Merrill Swain:

Minimal Pairs:

Modals:

Monitor Hypothesis:

Morphemes:

Morphology:

Nasals:

Natural Order Hypothesis:

Noam Chomsky:

Nonexplicit illocutionary force:

Nonliteral locutionary act:

Nouns:

Noun Phrase:

Object Complement:

Obstruents:

Onomatopoetic words:

Output Hypothesis:

Palatal Sounds:

Performative Verbs:

Phonetics:

Phonology:

Phrase Structure Rules:

Place of Articulation:

Polysemes:

Possessive Nouns:

Postalveolar Sounds:

Pragmatics:

Prefix:

Prepositions:

Prepositional Phrase:

Prescriptive Grammar:

Presupposition:

Pronouns:

Prototype:

Reference:

Referent:

Referent Image:

Relative Adverbs:

Relative Pronouns:

Scaffolding:

Second Language Acquisition:

Semantics:

Sentence:

Sentence Stress:

Silent Sounds:

Sonorants:

Speech Acts:

Stephen Krashen:

Stereotype:

Stops:

Subjacency Constraint:

Subject Compliment:

Sub-sentence:

Suffix:

Superlative Form:

Superordinate:

Surface Structure:

Synonyms:

Syntax:

Synthetic Truth:

Tensed Sounds:

Tensed Verbs:

Tensed S (Subject) Constraint:

Thematic Roles:

Transformational Rules:

Truth:

Unit Movement Constraint:

Untensed Sounds:

Velar Sounds:

Verbs:

Verb Phrase:

Voicing:

Vowels:

Wh-Movement:

Word Classes:

Word Stress:

Zone of Proximal Development:

Additional Terms

# ABOUT THE AUTHOR

Sarina Chugani Molina currently serves as faculty in the Department of Learning and Teaching at the University of San Diego. She has experience working with English Learners from a multitude of backgrounds both within the United States and in International contexts. She is the program coordinator and instructor of graduate level courses in the M.Ed. in TESOL, Literacy, and Culture Program. She has authored English as a Foreign Language textbooks series entitled, *Visual English* and most recently, *English for Global Citizens*. Her research interests include teacher development in TESOL, teaching English as a global language, and addressing social and educational inequities for students from culturally and linguistically diverse backgrounds.